DAVID GASCOYNE

A SHORT SURVEY OF SURREALISM

Preface by Dawn Ades

Introduction by Michel Remy

ENITHARMON PRESS

First published in November 1935
by Cobden-Sanderson

Published in this edition in 2000
and reprinted in 2003
by the Enitharmon Press
26B Caversham Road
London NW5 2DU

Distributed by Central Books
99 Wallis Road
London E9 5LN

Distributed in the USA and Canada
by Dufour Editions Inc.
PO Box 7, Chester Springs
PA 19425, USA

ISBN 1 900564 66 1 (paperback)
ISBN 1 900564 96 3 (cloth edition, limited to 50
signed and numbered copies, bound by The Fine Bindery)

British Library Cataloguing-in-Publication Data.
A catalogue record for this book is available
from the British Library.

Set in 10.5 Bembo by Bryan Williamson, Frome,
and printed in Great Britain by
Antony Rowe Ltd.

David Gascoyne was born in 1916 in Harrow, Middlesex, and educated at Salisbury Cathedral School and the Regent Street Polytechnic, London. His first collection of poetry, *Roman Balcony and Other Poems*, was published when he was sixteen, and in 1933 Cobden-Sanderson brought out his novel *Opening Day*. Both books are remarkable achievements for an adolescent, and they were followed by the equally striking poetry collections *Man's Life Is This Meat* (1936) and *Hölderlin's Madness* (1938), which established his reputation as one of the most original voices of the 1930s.

Gascoyne was among the earliest champions of Surrealism: in 1935 his *A Short Survey of Surrealism* was published, and in the next year he was one of the organisers of the London International Surrealist Exhibition. From this period, and during his time living in France in 1937–1939, date his friendships with Dalí, Max Ernst, André Breton, Paul Eluard and, later, Pierre Jean Jouve. As well as becoming internationally celebrated as a poet – especially after publication of his *Poems 1937–1942*, with its Graham Sutherland images – Gascoyne became highly regarded as a translator, notably of the leading French Surrealists.

After the war Gascoyne again lived in France (1947–48 and 1953–64), partly in Paris and partly in Provence. He consolidated his reputation with *A Vagrant and Other Poems* (1950) and with *Night Thoughts* (1956), commissioned by Douglas Cleverdon for BBC Radio. His *Collected Poems*, published by Oxford University Press in 1965, were reprinted six times. Enitharmon Press has recently published a substantial volume of Gascoyne's *Selected Poems*, as well as his *Selected Verse Translations*, *Selected Prose 1934–1996* and his novella *April*. David Gascoyne was made a Chevalier de l'Ordre des Arts et Lettres by the French Ministry of Culture for his lifelong services to French literature. He died in November 2001.

OTHER ENITHARMON BOOKS
BY DAVID GASCOYNE

Novalis: Hymns to the Night (1989)

Poems of Milosz (1993)

Selected Poems (1994)

Selected Verse Translations (1996)

Selected Prose 1934–1996 (1998)

Encounter with Silence: Poems 1950 (1998)

April: A Novella (2000)

ACKNOWLEDGEMENTS

The publisher would like to express warm thanks to Dawn Ades and Michel Remy for so expertly and eloquently placing *A Short Survey of Surrealism* into its artistic and literary context. Marco Livingstone and Roger Scott have very kindly given editorial guidance, and as always David Gascoyne and his wife Judy have been encouraging and hospitable while the book has been in preparation.

This new edition of the *Short Survey* has been made possible by a generous grant from the Trustees of the Elephant Trust – a charity established by Roland Penrose and Lee Miller. A special debt of gratitude is due to the Trust's energetic and sympathetic Secretary, Julie Lawson, who for many years has been a devoted friend to the Gascoynes and a strong supporter of the Enitharmon Press.

CONTENTS

PREFACE

A Short Survey of Surrealism is all too often absorbed into the history of the London International Surrealist Exhibition of 1936 and the creation of the Surrealist group in England. It is true that David Gascoyne (only twenty years old at the time, and a published poet) was on the organising committee of the Exhibition and a member of the group. But the *Short Survey* was published a year before the high profile Exhibition, which in Breton's view 'marked the highest point in the graph of the influence of our movement'. The gap is important, for it helps us to understand the special character of this document, its enduring value as history and as testimony of the movement's real life.

Of course *A Short Survey* was evidence of the growing international interest in Surrealism, but it was prompted not as part of an official launch but by a poet's conviction of the movement's overwhelming importance for the modern world and for poetry in its broadest sense. After 1936 the move was inexorably towards the dominance of the visual aspects of Surrealism as perceived by the public and to exhibitions as a primary mode of expression.

The balance between Surrealism's different manifestations in *A Short Survey* allows us to see it whole, not just as an art movement backed up by manifestos. This balance is based to a large extent on the early Surrealist reviews and books such as Breton's *Nadja.* The illustrations, twelve in all, have the same pointed and apposite effect as Gascoyne's prose; chosen with great precision, they include paintings, an object, a film still from *Un Chien andalou*, Man Ray's photograph of the dust breeding on Duchamp's Large Glass and Arp's string *Dancer*, but no 'primitive' art.

Gascoyne was in Paris in 1935 to research *A Short Survey*, commissioned from the publishers of his novel *Opening Day*, Cobden-Sanderson. His gifts as a translator led to a recommendation from Eluard to Dalí to render the latter's *Conquest of the Irrational* into English. No one has better caught the sparkling, exaggerated eloquence of Dalí's writing; first published by Julien Levy, this is the version that has appeared since 1942 in *The Secret Life of Salvador Dalí*, though without acknowledgement.

Gascoyne found Breton, Eluard and Hugnet generous with

guidance, publications and documents. But he was already independently familiar with Surrealism and writing Surrealist poetry as well as translating it. As a 16-year-old student at the Regent Street Poly, he had bought (from Zwemmers in Charing Cross Road) back copies of the founding journals *La Révolution surréaliste* (1924–29) and its successor *Le Surréalisme au service de la révolution* (1930–33), and of Eugène Jolas's *transition*; on his first trip to Paris in 1933 he purchased collections of poetry by Breton, Eluard, Tzara and others. All these he absorbed, and they provided the frame for the *Short Survey*. Of the current organ *Minotaure* (1933–39), though, he is wary, and he expresses reservations in the *Short Survey* about the Surrealists' collaboration on this 'magnificently produced but somewhat expensive review, well known in this country. Whether they consider it an advantage to appear side by side with Paul Valéry and articles on Cézanne I cannot say; but at any rate their work is now as well presented as it could be, with copious and finely produced illustrations.'

'Survey' is hardly an adequate term for this remarkable book. Although short, it is unhurried, spacious, and clear, unencumbered with tense compressions and generalisations. It encompasses not only Surrealism but also its ancestors, including Dada, with ample quotations from the manifestos and other books and poetry collections. Gascoyne knew that Surrealism was 'not a style, not a school of literature or painting, not a system of aesthetics'. Written from the inside, it is, like so many Surrealist books, an indefinable document, part history, part manifesto, part critique. The order, structure and language are so beautifully judged that one is barely aware of their role in carrying the reader to the heart of the movement. The introduction, standard place for general definitions, explanations and acknowledgements, starts instead with an extraordinary sentence, which is both a statement of faith in Surrealism and also a lucid commentary on the opening passages of Breton's first *Surrealist Manifesto* (1924).

Here and elsewhere Gascoyne implicitly reveals the internal trajectory of a movement that was never still or monolithic. So Chapter One on the 'Ancestors of Surrealism' opens with de Sade, 'object of revulsion and horror to a whole horde of petty moralists' and the 'starting point of the great Romantic movement that rolled across the last century like a theatrical thunderstorm'. De Sade is presented as a figure whom the Surrealists were then fighting to restore to serious attention as a revolutionary moralist and defender of the 'imagination of love', in Eluard's phrase. Thus Gascoyne sets up a to-and-fro movement between past and present that works in a comparable way, though here with a different application, to Breton's *Communicating Vessels*.

The idea of Surrealism as a linking vessel, 'a capillary thread or tissue' between different states, interior and external worlds, was what appealed above all to Gascoyne. He spoke of it as 'the finally unified world in which spirit and matter are no longer seen as in contradiction, and reason and imagination are no longer opposites, nor subjectivity and objectivity'.[1] This was the point of fullest agreement between them, but also the origin of their discord, over the sense in which 'spirit' was to be understood. The Surrealists were utterly set against any hint of religion, while increasingly Gascoyne was to feel the 'intolerable nature of human reality when devoid of all spiritual, metaphysical dimension'.[2]

The incident treated at greatest length in the *Short Survey*, however, was the Aragon Affair, which brought to a head the intransigence of the Communist Party vis-à-vis the Surrealists and the issue of writing politically, leading to Aragon's defection from Surrealism. This was an urgent issue for Gascoyne himself, then a member of the Party, which he criticises for 'making a silly mistake in treating [the Surrealists] either with scorn or suspicion simply because their work does not happen to be about strikes, hunger marches or life in the distressed areas'. He quotes with approval the 1934 pamphlet by Claude Cahun (also a Communist Party member), *Les Paris sont ouverts*, in which she argues that the 'most revolutionary experience in poetry under the capitalist régime' had been 'the Dadaist-Surrealist experience, in that it has tended to destroy all the myths about art that for centuries have permitted the ideologic as well as economic exploitation of painting, of sculpture, of literature, etc. . .'.

In the autumn of 1936 Gascoyne went to Barcelona with Valentine and Roland Penrose. His experience of the Communist Party there, the fact that they hated the Anarchists and the P.O.U.M. (the Trotskyists) more than Franco's Fascists, fed his disillusionment. In

---

[1] 1992 interview in *Stand*, from *Selected Prose 1934–96* (London: Enitharmon Press, 1998), p. 49.

[2] Introduction to *Selected Poems* (London: Enitharmon Press, 1994), p. xv.

spite of this, the lecture on Surrealism he gave in Oxford on his return to England is uncompromising in terms of its commitment to Communism but even more so to poetry and the lyrical imagination. He adopts Eluard's definition of poetry: 'Caprice, contradiction, violence . . . Perpetual struggle, life's very principle . . .' This has remained at the core of Gascoyne's attitude to poetry, and his non-conformity to the polite urbanity of certain English poetry: 'I prefer extremism, things which are on the margin, really: I still like Dada because it is anti-literature.'[3]

A Short Survey of Surrealism still stands out as a beacon in the massive literature on Dada and Surrealism. Rereading it recently I recognised its central, formative influence on my own approach to Surrealism. It has also served as a model to others, for instance for the 1978 exhibition *Dada and Surrealism Reviewed* masterminded by Gascoyne's old friend Roland Penrose. Poised at a critical moment of Surrealism between its first intense decade of intimate experiment and its flowering onto an international arena, *A Short Survey* is both a document of its time and an impeccable history of Surrealism for today.

DAWN ADES
London 2000

[3] Interview, *op. cit.*, p. 52.

THE ENTRANCE OF THE MEDIUM

When David Gascoyne turned into the rue de Tournon, just round the corner of his hotel, one bright day in July 1935, he could have had no idea that an important meeting was about to take place. Coming towards him was Paul Eluard, whom he already knew well, accompanied by an Englishman he had never met before, Roland Penrose. Penrose had been based in Paris since 1922 and had made friends with most of the French Surrealists. 'It was the encounter of two explorers who had discovered independently the same glittering treasure,' Penrose recalled of this meeting in his *Scrapbook*. Gascoyne asked him, 'Why do we know nothing of this in England?' adding, 'Something's got to be done!' With these words at the back of his mind when he returned to London in September 1935, Penrose embarked on the formation of a group of artists and art critics who 'shared our urgent desire to make clear to Londoners that there was a revelation awaiting'.[1] Nine months later, in June 1936, the International Surrealist Exhibition – on whose organising committee Penrose and Gascoyne sat – constituted a powerful and challenging materialisation of that urgency.

The presence in Paris of David Gascoyne, a young, tall, nineteen-year-old poet, was explained by the commission he had received from the publisher Cobden-Sanderson to write a survey of Surrealism, a movement which had already created some stir in London magazines and papers, especially on the occasion of exhibitions.[2] Gascoyne had already published a novel inspired by his adolescent years, *Opening Day* (Cobden-Sanderson, 1933), and with advance royalties from that he had been able to travel to Paris for the first time in autumn 1933, with Herbert Read's *Art Now* in his pocket. Back in London, he resumed his almost daily visits to David Archer's Parton

[1] Information collated from David Gascoyne's declarations, from the Afterword to his *Collected Journals 1936–1942* (London: Skoob Books, 1991), and from Roland Penrose, *Scrapbook* (London: Thames and Hudson, 1981), p. 56.

[2] Especially the Mayor Gallery mixed show of French and British artists in April 1933, the exhibition of Max Ernst's works at the Mayor Gallery in June 1933 – whose only champions were Paul Nash in the *Week End Review*, and Herbert Read in *The Listener* – and the exhibition of Salvador Dalí's drawings and paintings at the Zwemmer Gallery in May 1934.

Street Bookshop, where he met George Reavey, a brilliant poet and distinguished translator of Russian poetry, and, through him, Julian Trevelyan, a painter and printmaker who was to be a member of the British Surrealist group for a while. In his turn, when Gascoyne returned to Paris a few months later, Trevelyan introduced him to S. W. Hayter, the famous Surrealist painter and printmaker, and founder of Atelier 17, a workshop that served as a unique meeting point for young British artists arriving in Paris, and for confirmed artists such as Dalí, Miró or Ernst, who wanted to learn, or improve on, their own printmaking techniques.

David Gascoyne's entrance into the avant-garde art world was thus facilitated, and he visited the studios of Ossip Zadkine, Jean Hélion, Max Ernst, Vieira da Silva and Pavel Tchelitchew, in the process gathering information and material for the book he was to write a year and a half later. Upon his return to London, he also met Roger Roughton, a young poet deeply interested in the new developments in poetry, at David Archer's bookshop, shared a flat with him in Southwark and both joined to 'explore with excitement the current manifestations of "modernity" in literature and the arts',[3] writing poetry and contributing to literary periodicals. Among these, there was Geoffrey Grigson's *New Verse*, whose policy, since its inception in January 1933, was to defend poetry uncompromisingly as a force of protest and renewal in the face of conventional, conservative poetics. In October 1933, *New Verse* included Gascoyne's *And the Seventh Dream is the Dream of Isis*, the first English Surrealist poem ever published.

Curiously enough, it seems inevitable to see the rue de Tournon chance meeting in 1935 in the light of, and as a kind of direct, concrete answer to, the December 1933 *Minotaure* enquiry about encounters. The questions, devised by Breton and Eluard, had been: 'What was the most important meeting of your life?' and 'Up to what point did that meeting give you the impression of chance? of necessity?' This was a central issue for the Surrealists at the time; chance encounters and coincidences signified in themselves the short-circuiting of reason, the elision of all deliberate choices, and the crystallised expression of the secret laws of the subconscious. In these was recognised 'the marvellous precipitate of desire' – a desire which is

[3] David Gascoyne, 'Afterword', *Collected Journals*, op. cit., p. 345.

suddenly, magically made manifest. Gascoyne and Penrose's encounter was symptomatic of the silent, subterranean work of the Surrealist spirit.

It is also in close connection with this revelatory 'precipitation', I am convinced, that one has to see the abundance of related publications and coincidental events throughout 1935 – a year of radical defiance of the literary Establishment and 'Bloomsburyism'. In May 1935, David Gascoyne signed the 'First Manifesto of English Surrealism', published in French in Christian Zervos's *Cahiers d'Art*,[4] a large prestigious magazine which was for a while one of the voices of Surrealism. Presented as a 'fragment' – the full text from which it is supposed to have been extracted was never written – it wholeheartedly bases itself on Breton's propositions, pledges allegiance to dialectical materialism, to the Workers' International and the fight against Fascism, and vibrantly hopes that 'a vast field of poetic, artistic and philosophic action may open in England'.[5] In June 1935, on one of his frequent stays with Gala and Salvador Dalí in their recently-acquired large studio in the rue de l'Université on the Left Bank, Gascoyne spent two weeks translating Dalí's *Conquest of the Irrational*, which had just been published and attracted much attention from the Surrealists. The translation, which was accompanied with thirty-five reproductions, was printed in July in Paris and published by Julien Levy in New York. It is during that stay, on 19 June, that the dreadful news came to the three of them that René Crevel (who Gascoyne sadly never met) had committed suicide, one of the reasons being his desolation at the schism between the Communists and the Surrealists. That evening, Gascoyne, Dalí and Gala attended the Surrealist meeting held at the Café de la Place Blanche, at which Crevel's desperate gesture – and his being given a religious funeral – were discussed.

Among all the various individual attempts to renew the expression of the self by uncovering and opening the paths and slopes which lead

---

[4] June 1935, p. 106.

[5] It is relevant to remember that David Gascoyne accompanied Christian Zervos and Roland Penrose to Spain in October 1936. The idea was for Zervos to write a book which would show that the Republicans had in no way destroyed monuments or any national treasures in Catalonia. Gascoyne, then, worked for a while for Radio Catalonia.

to its unchartable depths, whether through writing or painting, mention must be made of 'Why the English Have no Taste' an article written by Herbert Read[6] and published in the then Surrealist, French magazine, *Minotaure* in June 1935; this was a rather scathing, definitive criticism of the English mentality and attitude towards art. To quote this regrettably little-known article at length will perfectly illustrate the context in which *A Short Survey* was written and published.

Basing his argument on the close interdependence of Puritanism and Capitalism which, by combining the religious and economic aspects of society, 'brought an end to our plastic modes of expression', Herbert Read further explains that 'every Englishman aspires' to 'a certain idea of normality', summed up 'in the terms *common sense* and *sense of humour*'. The former is 'the accepted opinion, agreed conventions, perfected habits' which 'the Englishman of the capitalist-puritan era endeavour[s] to attain'. As regards the latter, he sees 'English laughter' as 'not bodily laughter – not *belly* laughter, like the laughter of Chaucer and Rabelais', but 'mental laughter, caused by an unconscious disturbance of suppressed instincts', from which there also comes 'our so-called hypocrisy, which is not pure hypocrisy, just because it is unconscious; our prudishness, our coldness in love, our lack of wit'. This, he goes on, determines 'the prevalent indifference to the plastic arts . . . an anti-plastic tendency'. It is 'the fear of infringing the limits of normality [which] tends to inhibit such a mode of expression'. As a result, he concludes, to break the 'destructive mechanism of a mind exposed to criticism', one has to see that 'the cause of the arts is the cause of revolution':

---

[6] Herbert Read was among the very few art critics fully aware of the irresistible development of aesthetics. He was living in Hampstead and was neighbour to Henry Moore, Barbara Hepworth, Ben Nicholson, Paul Nash and John Piper, a 'gentle nest of artists'. He was the author of seminal books such as *The Meaning of Art* (1931), *Art Now* (1933) and *Art and Industry* (1934) and believed in the advent of a free society governed by love rather than law. For him, art and morals were indissolubly linked, art was the 'primum mobile' of man's intellectual and moral progress and the only means for man to break the shackles of conventionality and prejudices. Evidence of his being constantly attuned to changing times is provided by *Art Now*, the bible of all young artists then; each successive edition was careful to revise or qualify previous statements in the light of new aesthetic developments. It was almost natural that Roland Penrose, who had settled in Downshire Hill in Hampstead, met him upon his return from France in 1935.

> We in England have suffered the severest form of capitalist exploitation; we have paid for it, not only in physical horror and destitution, in appalling deserts of cinders and smoke, in whole cities of slums and rivers of filth – we have paid for it also in a death of the spirit. We have no taste because we have no freedom; we have no freedom because we have no faith in our common humanity.

Historically speaking, *A Short Survey*'s intransigent commitment to the Surrealist principles can evidently be taken as providing an unpremeditated, unilateral answer to Read's vibrantly committed assertions and analysis of the causes of the present situation; the following words at the end of the *Survey* will suffice:

> The great task of this century is that of revising the old scales of value in every field, of destroying worn-out customs and institutions and of constructing a form of society in which men may be able to make full use of all their faculties.

In England, that same year, the publication of *Petron*, first as an extract which appeared in the *Criterion*, then in book form by Dent, brought to the fore the radical personality of Hugh Sykes Davies. A Cambridge don, he had been a member of the Experiment group[7] in the late 1920s, which had strong links with France, especially through young artists such as Julian Trevelyan, Gerald Noxon and Humphrey Jennings; he had written an article on Homer and Giambattista Vico and was a specialist in Romantic literature. Six months after *Petron* came out, Davies was on the organising committee of the International

---

[7] Experiment was a group formed at Trinity College, Cambridge in 1928 by young intellectuals and artists such as Jacob Bronowski, Gerald Noxon, Humphrey Jennings, Julian Trevelyan, George Reavey and Hugh Sykes Davies. Though never departing from the belief in the necessity to keep intellectual standards, they sought to distance themselves from dominant moral codes and artistic labels, and liberate art and literature from aesthetic preconceptions. Julian Trevelyan's outcry 'TO DREAM IS TO CREATE' is evidence of the group's determination to explore the 'new reality'. They ran a magazine entitled *Experiment* (November 1928–Spring 1931), and were invited to contribute to Eugène Jolas's *transition*, published in Paris, thus reinforcing the intellectual links between France and England and anticipating the links which were to be developed by Surrealism.

Surrealist Exhibition. *Petron* is a novel of adventures all based on the slipping of reality into dream-like visions and the permanent drifting of its narrative stance: the episodes of the hedgekeeper who protests against Petron's disturbing the signposts by passing a string through his ears and drawing it through the nostrils, or of Petron crossing a landscape bathed in a beautiful crimson sunset, which actually proves to be the bloody mouth of a giant, are cases in point. Detecting the oneiric origins of the *displacement* at work throughout the 'story', David Gascoyne, in his review for *New Verse* in December 1935, summed up the book in this way:

> One cannot help wondering whether Petron is an interior hero, a projection of genuine obsessions and inner conflicts, or whether he is merely an ingeniously manipulated puppet, made to dance to a fantastic tune that Mr Davies once heard in a library.

Of course, what Gascoyne sensed, is that Petron (both as a book and as a character), is a precipitate of all these, a precipitate of dream activity and the liberating desire it expresses.

That same year, Len Lye, a New Zealand poet, painter and, above all, filmmaker, who worked with Humphrey Jennings regularly and was to become an early member of the Surrealist group in England, made the first film ever without a camera, and without any team or assistant. Painted directly onto the celluloid reel, *Colour Box*[8] was a 'direct' film whose technique opened the way to many further cinematic developments, which managed to alienate themselves from rationality and a conventional filmic approach.

Those years, and 1935 more particularly, were moments of great movement between France and England. Eileen Agar, who had worked in Paris under the guidance of a Czech Cubist artist, Frantisek Foltyn, went back there several times with her partner, Joseph Bard, an Austrian intellectual who knew most of the French artists and critics of importance; she visited Brancusi and met some of the Surrealists, developing an intimate friendship with Paul Eluard from 1934 onwards. Probably as a result of these contacts her style changed radically on her return to England, leaving more room for spontaneity and the lyricism of the imagination, and less to pure

---

[8] Len Lye, *Colour Box*, G.P.O. Film Unit (1935), 3 min.

formalism; she was encouraged in this direction by Paul Nash, whom she had just met. A kind of latent connection was established here too through her between those who were to be part of the Surrealist movement in Britain and the French Surrealists.

Indeed, the story of the introduction of Surrealism to Britain is almost the story of a kind of smuggling in of new aesthetics, among whose many agents can be counted John Banting (through his links with Nancy Cunard, Samuel Beckett, Aragon and Man Ray), Humphrey Jennings (an acquaintance of Man Ray and Eluard), Julian Trevelyan (who spent much time in S. W. Hayter's studio), and F. E. McWilliam (friendly with both Brancusi and Henry Moore). These artists' many successive stays in Paris could only consolidate the base on which Surrealism was being gradually constructed in Britain through various, scattered articles and exhibitions. The 'monument' – a most living one – was unveiled and fully revealed to the view of the English public on 11 June 1936 when the International Surrealist Exhibition opened at the New Burlington Galleries, Burlington Gardens, London W1.

Coincidentally or not, Gascoyne's *Short Survey* can be seen, then, as the detonator of all those high explosive charges, establishing the particularly high voltage of the new magnetic waves. It provided a frame, a focus for the new energy, putting into plain words, and inscribing within the history of twentieth-century ideas, the various challenges they represented to conservative, smug aesthetic isolationism and, beyond, to the prevailing hidebound conceptions of the life of man. From now on, if one may borrow the title of Gascoyne's volume of Surrealist verse published in February 1936, only six months after his *Short Survey*, 'man's life' will be 'this meat' . . .

The argumentative clarity and lucidity of purpose of *A Short Survey* are striking. The chronology is no mere list of dates; it is used to support the process of refinement at work in the evolution from Baudelaire, Rimbaud and Lautréamont to Dada and Surrealism. From behind the sequence of innumerable facts and events, faithfully and accurately recorded, there appears an insuperable logic, that of the vertiginous descent into the hidden recesses of the subconscious. Marking each stage with the names of those who participated, briefly or not, in the elaboration of Surrealist principles, and with extracts from seminal texts, Gascoyne manages to recreate the *drama* of Surrealism from its inception up to the mid-1930s in the field of aesthetics as well as politics – not separating one from the other. The historical importance of *A Short Survey* resides precisely in the sympathetic process of clarification which underlies it, and the landmark it constitutes in the art history of Britain. The successive internecine quarrels which caused splits and dissensions in the French Surrealist group, the aesthetic and moral values at stake in the political commitments of most of its members, the dialectical relationships between art and politics, emerge as pointers of aesthetic concepts entirely new in England and as signifiers of an investigation whose iconoclastic purpose was to combat the fossilisation of aesthetics. Simultaneously emphasis was laid upon the radical elusiveness of the undertaking, founded as it was on permanent self-questioning.

As a matter of fact, in the circumstantial listing of all the important articles published in *La Révolution surréaliste, Le Surréalisme au service de la révolution* and *Minotaure,* in the detailed list of publications by each and every French Surrealist, David Gascoyne draws the map of the natural inevitability of Surrealism. The final pages emphasise, by no great stretch of the imagination, both 'the strong Surrealist element in English literature' – a thread which, he insists, runs through the works of Shakespeare, Swift, Young, Blake, Beddoes, Lear and Lewis Carroll – and the fact that Surrealism basically transcends all narrow nationalisms. Indeed, in Gascoyne's view, Surrealism owes much both to German and Spanish thought and represents a dialectical synthesis of German writers (Hegel, Feuerbach, Engels and Marx) and the lyricism and imaginativeness of Southern cultures. The whole of *A Short Survey* has all the qualities of concrete vision: deeply rooted in factuality, in space and time, it also manages to rise above these categories and grasp Surrealism in the making.

As a coda to his text, Gascoyne included translations of ten Surrealist texts (four of them translated by Ruthven Todd) which illuminated points made in his account.[9] Already, prior to the publication of *A Short Survey, transition*, in May and August 1927, and *This Quarter*, in September 1932, both trans-Channel and transatlantic reviews, had been among the first literary magazines to print translations of Surrealist texts to the English public – altogether about sixty-

[9] There were, in addition, twelve plates of Surrealist paintings and photographs. The dust jacket was designed by Max Ernst in red and green and the gilt design on the front cover was by Yves Tanguy.

five texts. Those included in *A Short Survey* preceded the publication of other translations, such as Benjamin Péret's *Remove Your Hat* and the thirty poems in the June 1936 special issue of Roger Roughton's *Contemporary Poetry and Prose.*

Although some of the critics seem to have turned a blind eye to the book, *A Short Survey* had quite a good reception, notably from Cyril Connolly, whose enthusiastic article in the December 1935 issue of *The New Statesman and Nation* was symptomatically entitled 'It's got here at last!'[10] After the first run of about 2000 copies, it was reprinted in 1936, probably to coincide with the Exhibition, with a slight but significant alteration. Gascoyne's translation of Tristan Tzara's poem extracted from *L'Homme approximatif* had been removed upon Tzara's demand: he had threatened Gascoyne and Cobden-Sanderson with prosecution if a whole passage about Breton sarcastically calling one of Tzara's texts *Twenty Elucubrations of a Police Agent*, was not deleted. This Gascoyne complied with.

Gascoyne's direct involvement with Surrealism was to last approximately another year and a half: he last appeared in their midst on the occasion of the Surrealist Objects Exhibition at the London Gallery on Cork Street in November 1937, but not *in presentia.* He contributed an object to the Exhibition, and three prose poems to its slim catalogue. Interestingly, the object, *The Half-back's Honeymoon*, was constructed in London from notes sent by Gascoyne from Paris.

Then, especially with the impending threat of war and increasing psychological tensions, Gascoyne grew dissatisfied with Surrealist activity. More and more preoccupied with the onslaught of forces of negation and fragmentation, with the loss of spiritual centre and the fragmentation of the individual, he tried to find a way out, or at least to discover traces of hope and the possibility of regeneration in Kierkegaardian existentialism, in Christian symbology and hermeticist

---

[10] There were other reviews in the following: *Left Review*, Vol. 2, No. 4 (January 1936), by Hastings (an unequivocal welcome); *Criterion*, Vol. XV, No. 60, p. 507 (April 1936), by Brian Coffey (positive); *Scrutiny*, Vol. IV, No. 4 (March 1936), by Geoffrey Walton (waspish); *Times Literary Supplement* (4 January 1936), p. 10 (anon., brief but positive). Two other articles mentioned *A Short Survey*, but probably only after publication of the second impression of the book: M. F. Cullis, 'Recent Verse', *New English Weekly* (16 July 1936), p. 276, and Geoffrey Grigson, 'A Letter from England', *Poetry Chicago*, 49, 2 (November 1936), p. 101.

propositions. Gascoyne's poetry became haunted by all the ineffectuated virtualities of man, the constantly deferred presence of truth, the inaccessibility of the ultimate Presence, and the groping of Man through the forests of symbols supplied by various philosophies and systems of thought.

This obstinate, unending search is encapsulated in his later interest in the symbolic meaning of the alchemical quest, the transformation of poison into remedy or, more precisely, the search for the antidote lodged inside the poisoned fruit. Writing becomes, then, the simultaneous apparition and disappearance of traces. It is in this intrinsic restlessness, this endless self-questioning that the permanence of the Surrealist spirit resides, and runs deep down, rhizome-like, in Gascoyne's world view. In 1982, in the text he wrote as the preface to the catalogue of Roland Penrose's exhibition of recent collages,[11] he refers to Surrealism as an integral part of the quest which started with neolithic rock painting and aboriginal graffiti; he then emphasises that 'the Surrealist artist is the medium through whom what he allows to occur on his pictorial surface comes into existence in order to question us and make us aware of the presence of Mystery, as of the fact that all images continually conceal something Other while appearing to reveal what they represent'.

The cardinal point of David Gascoyne's work, as first indicated by *A Short Survey*, has never ceased to be the experience of Difference and the mercurial element at the core of its writing.

MICHEL REMY
Université de Nice

[11] 'Roland Penrose' in *Roland Penrose, collages récents*, catalogue of his exhibition at Galerie Henriette Gomès, Paris (12 November–30 December 1982), reprinted in *Roland Penrose, Recent Collages (A Commemorative Exhibition)*, A Gardner Centre Gallery touring exhibition, University of Sussex (3–31 May 1984), p. 10 and in David Gascoyne's *Selected Prose 1934–1996*, edited by Roger Scott and introduced by Kathleen Raine (London: Enitharmon Press, 1998), pp. 186–88.

INTRODUCTION

Confined from early childhood in a world that almost everything he ever hears or reads will tell him is the one and only *real* world and that, as almost no one, on the contrary, will point to him, is a prison, man – *l'homme moyen sensuel* – bound hand and foot not only by those economic chains of whose existence he is becoming every more and more aware, but also by chains of second-hand and second-rate *ideas*, the preconceptions and prejudices that help to bind together the system known (ironically, as some think) by the name of 'civilisation', is for ever barred except in sleep from that other plane of existence where stones fall upwards and the sun shines by night, if it chooses, and where even the trees talk freely with the statues that have come down for ever from their pedestals – a world to which the entrance has generally been supposed, up till now, to be the sole privilege of poets and other madmen. For it is undeniably true that the oneiric[1] domain is still regarded in very much the same way as was the erotic domain during the Victorian era. That the dream is useless, as escape from reality, the dreamer a self-indulgent and lazy person, is the accepted view of an overwhelming majority. How, then, can man reconcile himself to the fact that he spends more than a third of his life on earth in sleep, and that he spends the whole time of his sleeping in a world that his conscious mind so despises?

It is the avowed aim of the Surrealist movement to reduce and finally to dispose altogether of the flagrant contradictions that exist between dream and waking life, the 'unreal' and the 'real', the unconscious and the conscious, and thus to make of what has hitherto been regarded as the special domain of poets, the acknowledged common property of all. So far as the Surrealists themselves are either writers or painters, it is also at the same time their aim to extend indefinitely the limits of 'literature' and 'art' by continually tending to do away with the barrier that separates the contents of the printed page or of the picture-frame from the world of real life and of action.

Taking this attitude as our point of departure, we are bound sooner or later to envisage a conception of imaginative expression in general, and of poetry in particular, that is almost totally different from that

[1] The Greeks called the dream: 'όναρ, hence Onirus, the god of dreams.

most widely current in present-day England and America – countries where the vital issues of Surrealism have been persistently misrepresented and obscured from the moment when, not so long ago, the rumour of this strange new 'modern' movement first came to our ears.

Surrealism, profiting from the discoveries of Freud and a few other scientific explorers of the unconscious, has conceived poetry as being, on the one hand, a perpetual functioning of the *psyche*, a perpetual flow of irrational thought *in the form of images* taking place in every human mind and needing only a certain predisposition and discipline in order to be brought to light in the form of written words (or plastic images), and on the other hand, a universally valid attitude to experience, a possible mode of living. It is thus a restatement of the ancient and supposedly discredited notion of inspiration – with a difference. This lyrical element of human thought, the source of all authentic poetry, common to all men did they but realise it, is manifested in the plays of Shakespeare and in the ravings of lunatics in *Kubla Khan* and in Walt Disney's *Silly Symphonies*; in the paintings of Picasso and in popular picture-postcards. 'I say that there exists a lyrical element that conditions for one part the psychological and moral structure of human society' (I quote from André Breton), 'that has conditioned it for all time and that will continue to condition it. This lyrical element is up to this day, even though in spite of them, the fact and the sole fact of specialists.' And when it is said that the aim of Surrealism is to break down the barrier separating dream ('poetry') from reality, the irrational from the rational, that is also to say that its aim is to make this 'sole fact of specialists' familiar to everyone. Here we have the answer to the problem raised by the apparent contradiction between the artistic attitude of Surrealism and its declared political faith. It should by now be clear to Marxists that the Surrealist attitude is totally in accord with the Communist philosophy of dialectical materialism, with its insistence on the synonymity of theory and practice, and that only the imminence of proletarian revolution allows Surrealism to hope that its aims will ultimately be fulfilled. The Surrealist cause is the revolutionary cause – in spite of the Surrealists' bourgeois origin, in spite of the attitude of certain dogmatic Marxists towards such phenomena as Freudian psychoanalysis and the more complicated developments of modern literature and art, and in spite of such apparent compromises on the part of the Communists as the

Franco-Soviet pact and the recent rehabilitation in Russia of the bourgeois conception of the family.

* * *

In the pages that follow I intend to treat the subject by employing a roughly chronological order; this method may have its disadvantages, but by the time we have reached the position of Surrealism at the present moment, even the reader who has as yet only the haziest idea of what Surrealism means may, I hope, be able to realise its fullest implications. To the reader already acquainted with the Surrealist movement and with the development of French literature during the last century I must apologise for having to go over what must be familiar ground, for this book is intended to serve as an introduction to Surrealism rather than to be a work of criticism.

I think I may remark here that although I have entitled my first chapter *Ancestors*, this should not be taken to imply that Surrealism is anything but a 'latent state of mind, a human attitude in the widest sense of the word human.' Surrealism is *not* a style, it is *not* a school of literature or painting, it is *not* a system of aesthetics. Hence its origins are not to be found in any particular epoch, though a number of writers of the last century, particularly in France, provided the immediate impetus to those men who during the last ten or fifteen years have devoted their whole attention to it, have defined it and given it a name, and have considerably enriched both literature and painting, as well as the cinema, by their researches.

* * *

I should like to acknowledge my thanks to MM. Breton, Eluard and Hugnet for their kind assistance in providing me with much information and many documents and publications with regard to the Surrealist movement; acknowledgments should also be made to the Surrealist writers for permission to translate the poems, etc., at the end of this volume, and to the Surrealist painters for the photographs of their works that I have used as illustrations.

D. E. G.

July–September 1935

CHAPTER ONE

ANCESTORS OF SURREALISM

'Close your ears to the clatter of bayonets, the yelping of the cannons; turn aside your gaze from the changing tides of battles lost or won; and then you will see an immense shining and inexpressible phantom arise from the shadows; you will see dawning over a whole star-sown epoch the enormous and sinister figure of the Marquis de Sade.' Thus reads the homage of Swinburne to a writer whose mysterious and very potent influence stretches right across the nineteenth century and into our own. Reviled and persecuted by his contemporaries, an object of revulsion and horror to a whole horde of petty moralists since his death, the Marquis de Sade, thanks to a vague and rather doubtful sort of popularisation of psycho-pathology, is known to most people today merely by the fact that a certain sexual perversion bears his name. It was only quite recently that the moral and philosophic side of his writings began to receive the serious attention of certain men, particularly of the Surrealists. 'For having desired to restore to civilised man the force of his primitive instincts,' wrote Paul Eluard in an article published in the eighth number of the review *La Révolution surréaliste*, 1926, 'for having desired to set free the imagination of love and for having fought desperately for absolute justice and equality, the Marquis de Sade was shut up almost all his life in the Bastille, and in the prisons at Vincennes and Charenton. His work has been delivered to the flames or to the senile curiosity of pornographic writers, who make it their *duty* to misrepresent him. His name has become the synonym of cruel and assassin. Over his indomitable spirit all the diehards have drivelled.' Yet it is probable that he would have been content to know that, while regarded as foul monster by the mob, he has always had the admiration of poets. To them, and to certain others, it is as a revolutionary moralist that he stands supreme, and it is as such that he will continue to influence the thought of courageous men.[1]

---

[1] The reader wishing for further information should refer to Mr Geoffrey Gorer's excellent book, *The Revolutionary Ideas of the Marquis de Sade* (Wishart, 1934). He may be surprised to find, however, that when Mr Gorer refers to the influence

It is inevitable that a survey of Surrealism should begin by going back to Sade, for he was in many ways the starting point of the great Romantic movement that rolled across the last century like a theatrical thunderstorm. We are forced to admit that most of its funereal trappings, phantoms, ruins and orientalisms are as derelict and dusty by now as old stage scenery; but it must not be forgotten that it did produce in passing a few men of an importance and significance as startling as that of real lightning-flashes. Such were Sade, Baudelaire, Rimbaud, Lautréamont. A few minor figures also distinguished themselves – Bertrand, Borel, Nerval – by being the first to indicate in their works the existence of the enormous illogical world that the Surrealist movement has subsequently brought to light in a more thorough and systematic manner.

Louis Bertrand, the obscure author of a single work first published in 1836 under the title of *Gaspard de la Nuit*, was, I believe, the originator of the prose-poem – a form which he used exclusively and that later on was to be greatly developed and made use of by Baudelaire, Rimbaud, Lautréamont (whose *Chants de Maldoror* were written entirely in prose) and many others. Petrus Borel, a poet and novelist considerably influenced by Sade, is best known by his romance *Madame Putiphar*, an offspring of the novels of terror, or *romans noirs*, that were so much in vogue at the beginning of the century. He was known as 'the lycanthrope', and the portrait of him that appears in the 1832 edition of his *Rhapsodies* depicts him as a sombre and revolutionary figure clutching a dagger. Gérard de Nerval, who made his appearance a decade or so later, deserves more attention than I can give him here. His work is imbued with a very remarkable fantasy, owing to the fact that he himself was never very far from madness. This spirit of fantasy, of a very high quality – his 'Le Prince

---

of Sade on the Surrealists, he does so in the following terms: 'Today his most open disciples (though they completely caricature him) are the French surréelistes (*sic*) with their rather impotent desire for violence, both intellectual and physical.' In many other passages Mr Gorer attacks the ignorance and hence injustice of those who have slandered Sade, which makes it all the more reprehensible of him that he should in this case be guilty of the same faults. In any case, he should be reminded that M. Maurice Heine, Sade's most faithful modern editor and commentator, for whom he expresses much admiration, is himself a member of the Surrealist group, his name appearing among the signatories of the latest Surrealist manifesto.

d'Aquitaine à la tour aboli' is one of the most famous examples of 'pure' poetry in the French language – Nerval carried beyond the limits of written poetry into the realm of real life, wearing extraordinary clothes, leading a lobster about at the end of a blue ribbon, and so on. There is an admirable account of him in Mr Peter Quennell's *Baudelaire and the Symbolists*.

This brings us to Charles Baudelaire, undoubtedly one of the greatest poets of modern times, whose importance for us in this study lies not so much in his technical perfection, his masterly control of poetic style, as in his moral attitude. Once more I am able to quote from an article by one of the Surrealists:

> How was such a man, made as none other to reflect doubt, hatred, scorn, disgust, sorrow, able to manifest his passions to such a degree and to empty the world of its contents so as to accuse all the defeated beauties and smirched truths with it, so placid and so complacent? Why did he set himself the task of fighting with inflexible rigour against sane reality, against that slavish morality that ensures the happiness and peace of supposedly free men? Why did he oppose ready-made good with evil to be done, God with the devil, stupidity with intelligence, the motionless pure sky with clouds? Listen to him saying, and with what desperate violence, that he would be lying did he not declare that his whole self was in the book that he had written. In spite of solitude, in spite of poverty, in spite of illness, in spite of laws he declares it, he struggles on. All the powers of unhappiness are on his side. Perhaps there is some chance of winning? Will black and white triumph over grey and dirt? Will the avenging hand finish writing on the walls of the immense prison the accursed sentence that would make them crumble away? But the light is fading. The sentence is interminable. Baudelaire can no longer see the words, the precious, mortal words. He is wounded by his weapons. Once more he discovers what his own end must be. Where judges would have been powerless, his illness conquers. Baudelaire is dumb. Outside the walls the night begins to moan.
>
> Paul Eluard, 'The Mirror of Baudelaire',
> *Minotaure*, No. 1

It was Rimbaud who wrote: 'Baudelaire is the first seer, the king of poets, a true god. But the surroundings he lived in were too artistic, and his much-vaunted form is paltry. The inventions of the unknown call for new forms.' This deficiency of form Rimbaud attempted to make good in his own work. *Les Illuminations* should be recognised as the first flaring-up of that spirit of invention and search for novelty which distinguishes the 'modern movement'. But it was not only against old literary forms that Rimbaud revolted, it was against old stupidities, conventions, morality – the whole life of the epoch of capitalist prosperity in which he lived. His departure to Abyssinia even, regarded by some as a sign of defeat and submission, was an act of revolt, in spite of what certain Catholic writers and others, all intent on *whitewashing* this noble rebel, have attempted to read into the absolutely desperate words of *Une Saison en enfer.* The disgusting attempts to pervert everything that Rimbaud ever wrote, to make of him (as others have tried to make of Baudelaire) a Catholic *manqué,* went so far that in 1927 his memory was honoured, by the mayor and councillors of his home town that he loathed so much, with a bronze statue, brass bands playing and general celebrations.[2] The Surrealists did not hesitate on this occasion to publish a manifesto denouncing such amazing hypocrisy.

In a study of the current of thought leading up to the Surrealist movement it is difficult to separate the name of Rimbaud from that of Lautréamont, whose *Chants de Maldoror* was published in 1869, just four years before *Une Saison en enfer* was written. 'There are new shivers running through the intellectual atmosphere at this time,' wrote Lautréamont. It was true. '*Leaves of Grass* appeared in 1855. Hopkins's poems were written between 1862 and 1889. Lear's *Book of Nonsense* was first published in 1846. Lewis Carroll produced his works between 1870 and 1880, period also of *Maldoror* and *Une Saison en enfer* . . .'[3] And did not the first volume of *Kapital* appear in 1867?

Of the life of Isidore Ducasse, the self-styled Comte de Lautréamont, almost nothing is known. He is generally believed to have been born in Montevideo, South America, in 1846; to have come to Paris to receive his education and to have died there in 1870. All other details of his life must be matters of pure conjecture; no authentic records are known to exist. In this respect, the collected edition of his works published by Au Sans Pareil in 1927 is somewhat misleading; it contains a long preface by Philippe Soupault purporting to

[2] The monument to Rimbaud was originally put up in 1901, but was destroyed during the [First World] War.

[3] Charles Madge, *New Verse*, No. 14.

be the result of considerable research into contemporary documents and to reveal a great deal about Lautréamont hitherto unknown; most of these 'new facts', however, are pure fabrication, as was pointed out in a pamphlet, *Lautréamont envers et contre tout*, published shortly afterwards and signed by Louis Aragon, André Breton and Paul Eluard.

Lautréamont published only two works, *Les Chants de Maldoror* and a short book of criticism, *Poésies*. They leave no doubt whatever that he was a man of genius. *Les Chants de Maldoror* are best described as a debauch of the imagination. The extraordinary, the horrible, the grotesque, the absurd are carried by Lautréamont to such extremes as have never been reached before or since. Maldoror, the protagonist, is a modern reincarnation of the Devil on the most colossal scale; the theme of the book is his incessant combat with the Creator, who is presented as an indescribably revolting monster. Maldoror is the pride of intellect, the Creator is blind and bestial stupidity. In spite of the delirious nature of the whole book, however, everything, even in the wildest scenes, is described in a cold, precise, almost scientific prose. One section is devoted to a hymn (in prose) to the glory of geometry and mathematics. It seems evident that *Les Chants* were written more or less automatically, for on almost every page there are to be found the most remarkable spontaneous metaphors and images bearing a striking resemblance to those produced during the early phases of Surrealist writing fifty years later.

Lautréamont's only other work, *Poésies*, is of quite another nature and seems to have been written as though in reply to his earlier excesses. Sternly he criticises the Romantics, the 'Great Softheads' of his epoch; and brilliantly he epitomises the essentials of a *balanced* conception of poetry. It is only a very short book, but it contains the germs of a great many ideas that have been developed since his death. 'His work plays the part of lever in the evolution (of poetry) that is already taking place,' says Tristan Tzara in number four of *Le Surréalisme au service de la révolution*; 'for he demonstrates, far better than Hugo, that by a sort of verbal magic or incantatory verbalism, the reason is capable of transformation and logic of dissolution.'

> The attempts of the romantics, of Rimbaud, and the success of Lautréamont were not however realised immediately. There was still no coherent effort towards the irrational, the surreal. There was no communal effort. The too heavy chains with which prejudices and

laws weigh down the mind had still to be broken. A few men were little by little accomplishing this task and preparing the way. After Lautréamont, this effort lost its vigour. Rimbaud and Lautréamont were both isolated, to the discredit of their epoch, and their gestures only acquired meaning with time.

Guy Mangeot, *Histoire du Surréalisme*, 1934

Not altogether without importance in the evolution I am attempting to trace is the poetry of Stéphane Mallarmé, a disinterested experimentalist, the object of whose researches was to restore to words their pristine clarity and evocatory power. This he sought to do by means of typography, ingenious redisposition of syntax, omission of articles and pronouns, suppression of punctuation, and so on. The claim to our attention of his *manner* is undoubtedly far more important than that of his *matter*, which had not much to distinguish it from the stock-in-trade of symbolist poetry, of which his *Après-midi d'un faune* is a classic example. Mallarmé's *Un Coup de dés* represents the extreme expression of his syntactical experiments, and is necessarily very obscure, if not entirely incomprehensible.

Two other minor nineteenth-century French poets who should not be passed over without mention are Germain Nouveau and Charles Cros. These two poets, both of whom were friends of Rimbaud in his turbulent Paris café days, have fallen into a regrettable obscurity, but some of the poems they have left are of such genuine and original beauty that it is not likely that they will ever be entirely forgotten. Of the life of Cros I know nothing save a few anecdotes connected with Rimbaud, and of Nouveau I know only that he led the life of a tramp and spent his last days as a beggar outside the doors of a church somewhere in the Midi. And of their poems I am hardly qualified to speak, as I am acquainted with only a very few of them. I only know that I shall never forget hearing Paul Eluard read, in his inimitable voice, the poem of Cros that tells of a tall white wall with a ladder against it, a herring lying on the ground, and one who came with a heavy hammer, a long piece of string and a nail; who mounted the ladder and nailed the string to the top of the wall, tying the herring to the other end; and then climbed down and went far, far away, leaving the herring slowly swaying there ever after. . . .

Then there is J. K. Huysmans, author of that extraordinary and apparently demodé novel, *A Rebours*, to which, unfortunately, we owe most of that literature known in England as 'the nineties'. But as has been pointed out before, if Oscar Wilde's *Portrait of Dorian Gray* is a reflection of Huysmans, it is only a very pale and distorted one. Huysmans should be judged by his own standards and not by those of his imitators. I quote from Havelock Ellis:

> Huysmans, with the intellectual passion of the pioneer in art, deliberate and relentless, has carried both the theory and the practice of decadence in style to the farthest point. In practice he goes beyond Baudelaire, who, however enamoured he may have been of what he called 'the phosphorescence of putrescence', always retained in his own style much of what is best in the classic manner. Huysmans' vocabulary is vast, his images, whether remote or familiar, always daring – 'dragged', in the words of one critic, 'by the hair or by the feet, down the worm-eaten staircase of terrified Syntax' – but a heart-felt pulse of emotion is restrained beneath the sombre and extravagant magnificence of this style, and imparts at the best that modulated surge of life which only the great masters can control.

It will not be inappropriate to quote here a passage from *A Rebours* describing the work of an artist who clearly foreshadowed the paintings of certain Surrealists:

> Des Esseintes had a special weakness for the other frames adorning the room. They were signed: Odilon Redon. They enclosed inconceivable apparitions in their rough, gold-striped pear-tree wood. A head of Merovingian style, resting against a bowl, a bearded man, at once resembling a Buddhist priest and an orator at a public reunion, touching the ball of a gigantic cannon with his fingers; a frightful spider revealing a human face in its body. The charcoal drawings went even further into dream terrors. Here, an enormous dice in which a sad eye winked; there, dry and arid landscapes, dusty plains, shifting ground, volcanic upheavals catching rebellious clouds, stagnant and livid skies. Sometimes the subjects even seemed to have borrowed from the cacodemons of science, reverting to prehistoric times. A monstrous plant on the rocks, queer blocks everywhere, glacial mud, figures whose simian shapes, heavy jaws, beetling eyebrows, retreating foreheads and flat skulls, recalled the ancestral heads of the first quaternary periods, when inarticulate man still devoured fruits and seeds, and was still contemporaneous with the mammoth, the rhinoceros and the big bear. These designs were beyond anything imaginable; they leaped, for the most part, beyond the limits of painting and introduced a fantasy that was unique, the fantasy of a diseased and delirious mind.

I like to think that were Des Esseintes alive today he would have a special weakness for the paintings of Salvador Dalí, whose horrors easily surpass those of Redon while at the same time their author manages to exercise a kind of clinical control over his imagination, thus preventing it from dragging him with it into domains from which it would be impossible to return.

★ ★ ★

The masterpiece of Alfred Jarry, *Ubu Roi*, was first produced in 1888, when the author was fifteen. This is an almost unequalled example of precosity, for there is nothing in the least innocent or childlike about the brutal satire of *Ubu*. It is difficult enough to give the English reader a very clear idea of the character of this play, with its particularly Gallic humour. Ubu, like the Creator in *Maldoror*, is a monster,[4] representing, under the guise of the most far-fetched cruelty and stupidity, the forces of bourgeois law, order and respectability. Anyone in Ubu's realm whose ideas or behaviour happened to be even slightly beyond the stunted comprehension of the king and his courtiers was immediately hurried off to prison or the scaffold. It is hardly surprising that society was loathe to recognise its apish face in Jarry's mirror, and that the play enjoyed great success as a farcical burlesque, and even today can still draw crowded and enthusiastic audiences in France (there was until recently an Alfred Jarry Theatre in Paris), where the public by this time probably understands full well at whom the fun is being poked but, owing to a curious feature of French psychology, seems rather to enjoy having its face heartily slapped occasionally.

Jarry's humour is not unlike that demonstrated by Wyndham Lewis in *The Wild Body* – a cold cerebral humour at the expense of the stupid and clumsy human machine. The laughter it produces performs the moral function of a purge; while at the same time it is antisocial and subversive. The Surrealist sense of humour – at its best, perhaps, in the poems and stories of Benjamin Péret – has undoubtedly developed from that of Jarry, who in his later works, particularly in the novel *Le Surmâle*, and in *Gestes et opinions du Dr.*

---

[4] 'If he resembles an animal he has above all a porcine countenance, with a nose like the upper jaw of a crocodile, and the general effect of his cardboard armour is to make him in every way the brother of that most aesthetically horrible of all marine creatures, the *linule*.' (Jarry)

Faustroll, pata-physicien, carried this element of humour into the domain of the purely irrational and absurd.

It is interesting to note that while the work of Jarry is not entirely confined to humour, even in the most lyrical of his poems, those contained in *Les Minutes de sable memorial,* for example, the humorous element is never far absent. A trace of it is even to be found in the magnificent poem *Le Sablier,* which begins:

> Suspends ton coeur aux trois piliers,
> Suspends ton coeur les bras liés,
> Suspends ton coeur, ton coeur qui pleure
> Et qui se vide au cours de l'heure
> Dans son reflet sur un marais.
> Prends ton coeur aux piliers de grès.

In the work of Jarry, more than almost any other writer, is to be seen the subtle interplay of humour and lyricism, never entirely divorced from one another and both proceeding in the beginning, I believe, from a common source.

Humour is also to be found, though under another aspect, in the curious writings of Raymond Roussel, who published his first work, *La Doublure,* a poem, in 1897. The life of this man, who died only in 1933, was quite as extraordinary as his books. The stories about him are innumerable, and out of them a veritable Roussel legend has grown. He was so rich that he could gratify, if he so wished, the least whim of his phenomenally fertile imagination. He went more than once round the world, and travelled round Europe and Asia Minor in the most luxurious motor caravan, fitted with studio, bedroom and bathroom: and yet was later able to boast that he had never used even the least of his travelling experiences as material for his writings, which consisted entirely of fantasy and invention. His wealth enabled him to put on the Paris stage a series of plays – *Locus solus, Poussière de soleils, L'Etoile au front* – and to employ the best-known music-hall artists to act the chief parts in them. Every performance created a scandal. The interminable recitals of minutely detailed anecdotes, the violent and insulting speeches, the introduction on the stage of the most far-fetched mechanical contrivances, the long incomprehensible pantomimes of moving statues, floating wreaths and glass flowers bobbing up and down – no audience could be expected to take such things quietly. No doubt he was to some extent engaged in pulling the public's gentle leg; but that does not exclude the possibility that he had a certain genius. There is real pleasure to be found in the pages of *Impressions d'Afrique*, for example. Roussel's Africa, of course, is an entirely imaginary one; he is said to have been inspired to write this book by a little pair of opera-glasses in his possession, one tube of which revealed painted on the lens the bazaars of Cairo, the other, Luxor. Here, as in his other works, are to be found long and apparently irrelevant anecdotes, descriptions of performances and ceremonies, inventions such as an orchestra of musical sponges, and so on. Nothing has ever rivalled in complexity or novelty the astounding inventions of Roussel: rails made of calves' lights; an immense diamond full of water and containing, among other things, a nude dancer with musical hair, a hairless cat, and a pointed metal horn pierced with holes; an immense glass cage in which historical episodes are enacted; packs of tarot cards containing emerald insects that emit halos capable of passing through flesh; a cock that writes the name of a woman on a sheet of ivory by coughing up blood on to it – all are described with a hairsplitting accuracy that enables us to see them as though they actually existed. They form, as Salvador Dalí has said, 'a dreamed itinerary of new paranoiac phenomena.'

Finally, we come to Guillaume Apollinaire, a man whose energetic enthusiasm was one of the main driving forces behind the beginnings of what is known as 'the modern movement', a term that is meaningless enough now but that comprised during the few years before the [First World] War, Apollinaire's heyday, all the new ideas and styles that have revitalised art in our time. He was a first-rate poet, he was the friend of all the new painters experimenting in Paris (and among the first to recognise the genius of such men as Picasso and Braque), he was a collector of negro sculpture at a time when the merits of negro sculpture were entirely unrecognised by collectors, he was editor of a selected edition of Sade, and, above all, he was the inspirer of all the young men about him. All the new movements of his time, Cubism, Futurism, Dadaism, found in him their staunchest champion; and no doubt he would have championed Surrealism, even without fully understanding it, had he lived to see it born. One of his last works, *Les Mamelles de Tirésias*, a play first performed in 1917, the year before his death, was subtitled: *drame surréaliste*. But another seven years were still to pass before the appearance of the first Surrealist manifesto.

CHAPTER TWO

THE DADAIST ATTITUDE

The word Dada means *hobby-horse.* It was not chosen for any reason; it simply happened to be the first word to meet the eye upon the page of a dictionary opened at random.

'I affirm that Tristan Tzara discovered the word Dada on the 8th of February, 1916, at 6 o'clock in the evening,' says Hans Arp, one of the first members of the group; 'I was there with my twelve children when Tzara pronounced for the first time this word, which aroused a legitimate enthusiasm in all of us. This took place at the Terrace Café in Zurich, and I had a roll of bread up my left nostril. I am persuaded that only imbeciles and Spanish professors can be interested in dates. What interests us is the dada spirit, and we were all dada before Dada began. . . .'

Negativism, revolt, destruction of all values, Dada was a violent protest against art, literature, morals, society. It spat in the eye of the world. Life is a disgusting riddle, but we can ask harder ones, was the Dadaist attitude. To many intelligent men at this time, suicide seemed to be the one remaining solution to the problem of living, and Dada was a spectacular form of suicide, a manifestation of almost lunatic despair.

Dada was the concrete expression of an almost universal state of mind, a state of mind that had existed even before the outbreak of the [First World] War. Marcel Duchamp's masterpiece, *The Bride Stripped Bare by her Bachelors, Even* was begun in 1911, for instance. (This profoundly enigmatic work, for which hundreds of notes and rough sketches were made, consists of a painting on glass of an enormous and incomprehensible machine.) Marcel Duchamp, always remaining aloof and refusing to enter into any organised activity, either Dadaist or Surrealist, exercised a deeper influence over the Dada movement than almost anyone.

Another typical example of this state of mind was Jacques Vaché, who committed suicide in 1918. A sophisticated anarchist, a type much resembling André Gide's Lafcadio, Vaché was Dada in his life rather than in anything he produced, for he was neither an artist nor a writer. In 1916 he came in contact with André Breton in a hospital at Nantes, and he seems to have had at that time a considerable influence over the future leader of the Surrealist movement, who later edited his remarkable and very moving letters from the front.

The Dada spirit was something shared by a number of extreme individualists of various nationalities, all of whom were in revolt against the whole of the epoch in which they lived. There is hardly a better expression of it than these words of Ribemont-Dessaignes: 'What is beautiful? What is ugly? What is great, strong, weak? What is Carpentier, Renan, Foch? Don't know. What am I? Don't know. Don't know, don't know, don't know.'

* * *

Zurich, during the [First World] War, was full of refugees from Central Europe. There were German pacifists, Hungarians, Romanians, Russian revolutionaries. Lenin himself was there, and could be seen playing draughts in the cafés. The general atmosphere was certainly political, but there were also a few writers and artists, Cubists, Futurists and Expressionists, among the emigrés. Towards the end of 1915 a young Romanian, distinguished so far by nothing but the fact that he had studied philosophy, arrived in their midst. This was Tristan Tzara, the future author of the first Dada manifesto and virtual director of the entire movement. Very soon after he was joined by an Alsatian poet and artist, Hans Arp, who came from Paris, where he had been working, not wishing to join in the War on either the French or the German side. These two men very soon became friends and about the same time they got to know a young German poet, Hugo Ball, and another Romanian, Marcel Janco. At the beginning of the following year another German poet, Richard Huelsenbeck, arrived in Zurich, and in February, as has already been described, the Dada movement began.

Hugo Ball opened the Cabaret Voltaire, a sort of café where pictures were exhibited, poems read and concerts given by a balalaika orchestra. On the 30th of March a 'magnificent concert of negro music' was given there, organised by Tzara, and Tzara, Huelsenbeck and Janco gave a simultaneous reading of their poems. Neither music nor poems showed the least trace of negro influence, of course; that was simply a current Dada expression. The poems that Tzara was writing at that time, typical Dada poems, were like this:

in your inside there are smoking lamps
the swamp of blue honey
cat crouched in the gold of a flemish inn
boom boom
lots of sand yellow bicyclist
chateauneuf des papes
manhattan there are tubs of excrement before you
mbaze mbaze bazebaze mleganga garoo
you turn round rapidly inside me
kangaroos in the boat's entrails. . .

In June 1916 appeared the first number of a review called *Cabaret Voltaire.* It published poems by Tzara, Huelsenbeck, Ball, Emmy Hennings (Ball's wife), Janco and others, including Guillaume Apollinaire, Blaise Cendrars and Marinetti.

Then the Cabaret Voltaire had to close down, to be replaced shortly afterwards by a Dada Gallery, where exhibitions of the work of such painters as Paul Klee, Kandinsky, Arp, Max Ernst, Giorgio de Chirico, Modigliani and Prampolini were given, and where, on the 14th of July, Tzara read his first Dada manifesto, attacking all values and ridiculing art, science, philosophy and psychology. Confusion reigned.

A year later appeared a second review, this time entitled *Dada I, recueil littéraire et artistique.*

While Dada was being born in Zurich, much the same thing was happening in New York. Marcel Duchamp was there at that time, teaching French; Francis Picabia was there, and so was Man Ray. Duchamp brought out two numbers of reviews, one called *Rongwrong*, and the other *The Blind Man*. Picabia contributed to a review entitled *Camera Work*, which was edited by Alfred Stieglitz, the owner of the Stieglitz Gallery. It was the street number of this gallery which gave Picabia the title of the review he founded a little later on, *291.*

Such was Marcel Duchamp's disgust for 'art' that he invented a new form of expression, which he called *ready-made.* A ready-made was any manufactured object that the artist liked to choose. For instance, in 1917 he sent in to the New York *Salon des Indépendants* a simple marble lavatory-bowl, which he entitled *Fountain*, signing it *R. Mutt.* (Needless to say, it was rejected.) And then again, he once took a little laundry-calendar picture, a mediocre little picture representing a woodland glen, painted in a couple of tiny bottles hanging like electric-light bulbs from the branches of two trees, one bottle red, the other green, and called it *Pharmacie*. Certainly Duchamp is one of the most extraordinary men alive. He is a champion chess-player, among other things; and it is said that in his apartment he has had a special door built, with two doorways, so that it is always both open *and* shut.[1]

Francis Picabia, a somewhat less interesting person than Duchamp, was a great asset to the Dada movement on account of his wealth of humour – a bitter and obscure sort of humour, to be sure, but nevertheless *humour* – and his indefatigable zest for bringing out reviews. In January 1917 he left New York for Barcelona, and there be brought out the first number of *391*, twelve numbers of *291* having already appeared. From Barcelona he went to Geneva, where he brought out a few more numbers of his review (which, for the most part, he wrote and illustrated himself) and also one or two small books of poems and drawings. And then, at last, he went on to Zurich, met Tzara and his friends and became merged into the Dada movement proper. He was known to the others as the Anti-painter, just as Tzara was known as the Anti-philosopher. He soon brought out the eighth number of *391* (February 1919), a completely Dada number this time, containing poems and prose by Picabia and Tzara, a manifesto by Gabrielle Buffet, Picabia's wife, and illustrations by Arp and Alice Bailly. On the cover was printed the following terse little verse by Picabia:

> I have a horror of the painting
> of Cézanne
> it bores me stiff.

Dada was in full swing in Zurich during 1919. Three numbers of the review *Dada* had already appeared, with contributions from Paris, where the movement was already growing. Tzara had published his *25 Poèmes*, illustrated with woodcuts by Arp. There were exhibitions,

---

[1] 'I have in mind the occasion when Marcel Duchamp got hold of some friends to show them a cage which seemed to have no birds in it but to be half-full of lumps of sugar. He asked them to lift the cage and they were surprised at its heaviness. What they had taken for lumps of sugar were really small lumps of marble which at great expense Duchamp had had sawn up specially for the purpose.' (André Breton, *Les Pas perdus*)

there were *soirées*. In April a particularly scandalous public *soirée* took place, during which five people dressed in stovepipes, which concealed their entire bodies, performed a dance entitled *Noir Cacadou*; a poet called Serner, it having been announced that he was going to give a reading of his works, came on to the platform and laid a bunch of flowers at the feet of a dummy figure; then Tzara got up to read a Dada proclamation, but by this time the whole hall was in such an uproar that no one could hear a word.

In May, *Dada 4–5* appeared, under the title of *Anthologie Dada*, containing work by almost all the Dadaists then known. And at the end of the year, Tzara left Zurich for Paris.

★ ★ ★

Before going on to describe the great days of Dada in Paris, 1920–21, I must mention the activities of Dada in Germany.

In Berlin a Dada group was founded by Richard Huelsenbeck, who returned there from Zurich in 1917. He published three reviews: *Club Dada* [1918], *Der Dada* [1919–20], and *Dada Almanach* [1920]. Among the contributors was George Grosz, whose pictures – violent, vitriolic attacks on modern society – are well known everywhere today. Francis Picabia and the Paris Dadaists also appeared in these reviews. In 1920 Huelsenbeck organised an enormous Dada show at Berlin, comprising one hundred and seventy-four exhibits.

In Hanover, Kurt Schwitters, a young poet and artist, founded a kind of Dadaism to which he gave the name of *Merz*.

But by far the most sensational of the German Dadaist groups was that of Cologne, where Max Ernst, the painter, and Johannes Theodor Baargeld, Communist poet and artist, founded *Der Ventilator* [1918], a Dada publication with strong social (or rather, anti-social) tendencies. In 1919 Ernst published an album of extraordinary drawings, entitled *Fiat Modes*, and in 1920, in collaboration with Hans Arp, his first collection of *collages* – (pictures cut from magazines, newspapers, etc., and stuck together in fantastic combinations) – entitled *Fatagaga*, short for 'Fabrication of guaranteed gasometric pictures'. In 1920, also, was held the Cologne Dadaists' exhibition, which created such a scandal that it had to be closed down by the police. In order to enter the gallery one had to pass through a public lavatory. Inside, the public was provided with hatchets with which, if they wanted to, they could attack the objects and paintings exhibited. At the end of the gallery a young girl, dressed in white for her first communion, stood reciting obscene poems. Destruction and sacrilege, not at all uncommon features of the feverish atmosphere of Germany immediately after the War.

In 1922, Max Ernst left Cologne for Paris, where he has remained ever since.

* * *

It is not surprising that Tristan Tzara found Paris, in 1920, the perfect headquarters for the Dada movement. It was there that all the most advanced and revolutionary forms of writings and painting were fermenting in one great melting-pot. Of all the movements that came out of it, Surrealism is the only one still alive today, and that is because it is fundamentally a revolution of ideas and not of the forms expressing them.

Three reviews of distinctly Dada tendency had already appeared in Paris. The first, founded by Pierre Albert-Birot in January 1916, was called *SIC*, with the sub-title: SOUNDS–IDEAS–COLOURS–FORMS. This was followed in 1917 by *Nord-Sud*, in which appeared André Breton, Philippe Soupault and Louis Aragon, future Surrealists, as well as Guillaume Apollinaire, Pierre Reverdy (the editor), Max Jacob and others, writers more affiliated with Cubism. The third review to appear was *Littérature* (which really meant Anti-literature), directed by Breton, Soupault and Aragon, and introducing for the first time the work of Paul Eluard. All these young men were in a very troubled and chaotic state of mind. They wanted to break everything down in order to liberate – what? They did not know as yet. When, in 1917, Guillaume Apollinaire showed him for the first time the publications of the Zurich Dadaists, it seemed to Breton that Dada was what he was out for. For some time he and his friends were enthusiastic supporters of the movement, but in the end they were to find it unsatisfying. Complete anarchy, such as Dada represented, ultimately amounts to the most restricting kind of tyranny.

Tzara was received with great enthusiasm by the *Littérature* group, and shortly after his arrival a Dada *matinée* was organised at a hall called the Palais des Fêtes. To open the performance, poems were read. Jean Cocteau read a few poems by Max Jacob, though neither of them were really Dadaists. The public, feeling sure that there was something outrageously 'modern' but 'clever', you know, all the same, was inclined to be admiring. Then Breton brought on to the platform a blackboard on which Picabia had drawn some kind of machine, and immediately proceeded to rub the picture off with a cloth. He then produced a picture by Marcel Duchamp, which was nothing more or less than a large printed reproduction of the Mona Lisa with a handsome pair of moustaches painted on to her face and bearing underneath the inscription: L.H.O.O.Q. (phonetic, perhaps, for 'Look!', since Duchamp knew English quite well).* By this time the public was beginning to get rather annoyed, and when Tzara, having announced a Dada manifesto, began to read a newspaper article to the accompaniment of the ringing of electric bells, the performance came to an end amidst general uproar and scandal.

At this time, most of the 'advanced' painters in Paris, Cubists and so on, belonged to a group known as the Section d'Or. They all found the phenomenon of Dada extremely disturbing. What would be the good of any kind of painting, once the Dada spirit got a wide hold? Dada scoffed at all forms of seriousness, but particularly at serious art. So the Section d'Or called a meeting on the 25th of February, 1920, at that famous café La Closerie de Lilas, with the object of 'expelling' the Dadaists. There was a great scene, as can well be imagined, for the Dadaists themselves were all present, and were not going to allow themselves to be 'expelled' by anybody without a good deal of protest. In a very short time the meeting degenerated into a shouting match; the tumult became so great that the *patron* of the café ordered the lights to be turned out, which made no difference, for the expulsion continued in the darkness. Léopold Survage climbed on to a chair and shouted: 'Ex-pelled! You are all ex-pelled!' Not that the Dadaists cared in the least whether they were or not.

Meanwhile, Dada became the fashionable topic of the day. The public wanted to understand. They wanted Dada explained to them. Was it a new system of ideas, a new form of expression? Was Dada serious, or was it simply a large-scale leg-pull? – But they were all on the wrong track. Dada expressed nothing but revolt: it was delirium, the public could never understand it unless they felt the same way themselves.

---

* Editor's note: This is in fact known to be a pun on 'Elle a chaud au cul' (she has a hot arse), which Duchamp described as 'a very risqué joke on the Gioconda'.

Dadaist books, reviews, periodicals, pamphlets continued to appear. Dadaist *soirées* were given at the Indépendants and the Université Populaire. On the 26th of May 1920 a Dada Festival was held at the Salle Gaveau, one of Paris's most famous concert-halls.

The Dada Festival may very well be regarded as the climax of the whole movement. Never was any audience presented with such a manifestation of out-and-out nihilism; certainly not in surroundings such as the rather prim Salle Gaveau, long accustomed to Bach concerts and organ recitals. The indignation of the public rose to more sublime heights than ever before. It is surprising that the police were not called in to intervene. On occasions such as these, of course, the behaviour of the audience was all part of Dada.

'Personal appearance of Charlie Chaplin', the advertisements announced. On the programme was printed the note: 'The Dadaists will pull their hair out in public.' But somehow or other neither of these parts of the performance took place. The following numbers were, however, presented:

The Sex of Dada.
Boxing Without Tears, by Paul Dermée.
Bold Behaviour, by Paul Eluard.
The Interloping Navel, music by G. Ribemont-Dessaignes.
Presbyterian Festival Manifesto, by Francis Picabia.
The International Crook, by André Breton.
The Second Adventure of Monsieur Aa, the Anti-pyrine, by Tristan Tzara.
You will forget me, Sketch, by André Breton and Philippe Soupault.
The American Nurse, music by Francis Picabia.
Frontier Dance, by G. Ribemont-Dessaignes.
System DD, by Louis Aragon.
Symphonic Vaseline, by Tristan Tzara, played by 20 people.
The Celebrated Illusionist, by Philippe Soupault.

As at the performance given at the Indépendants, the Manifesto was simply an excuse to hurl insults and abuse at the audience, who were not slow, this time, to respond. During one of the intervals a party of young people went out to a nearby butcher's shop and came back armed with pieces of raw meat, which they did not hesitate to fling on to the stage as soon as the performance was resumed. Tomatoes, also, flew through the air, squashing against the gilded columns of the hall and splashing everybody, including the owner of the building, Madame Gaveau, who was sitting, furious, in a box. The Dadaists on the platform were delighted and flung the missiles back at the audience. The Festival became a battle, and the Press decided, afterwards, that Dada was sacrilegious, subversive and altogether outrageous, which was precisely what it was intended to be.

* * *

It would be impossible to summarise here all the more or less hectic antics of the Dada reviews. There were so many of them; they sprang up in a night, lasted for two or three numbers and then gave place to others. The only reviews to have appeared fairly regularly seem to have been Breton's *Littérature*, Picabia's *391*, Eluard's *Proverbe* (six issues) and Tzara's various publications. Of the innumerable contributions to these papers one might cite as being typically Dada: Picabia's ink-blot entitled *La Sainte Vierge*; Aragon's poem *Suicide*, consisting of the letters of the alphabet; Tzara's bus-tickets (stuck to the page, a different one for every copy) entitled *Douleur en cage dada à la nage*; the photograph of a gollywog entitled *Natures Mortes, Portrait de Cézanne, Portrait de Rembrandt, Portrait de Renoir*, and Breton's poem consisting of an extract from the telephone directory. A very comprehensive survey of the whole of Dada by Georges Hugnet has been published serially in *Cahiers d'Art*.

One can well imagine the Paris background to all this, the first feverish outbreak of post-war irresponsibility, a great deal of money flowing in all directions, Americans arriving in hordes, endless talking and drinking in every café from Montmartre to Montparnasse. The favourite café of the Dadaists was a bar called Certa in the Passage de l'Opéra, described by Aragon in his *Paysan de Paris*:

> Here the word Dada is understood rather differently than elsewhere, and with more simplicity. It means neither anarchy nor anti-art nor any of the things that made the journalists so timid that they preferred to call this *movement* by the name of *hobby-horse* (Cheval d'enfant). To be Dada is no dishonour, it means simply a group of habitués, rather noisy young people sometimes, perhaps, but *sympathiques* nevertheless. One says: a Dada, as one says: the fair-haired gentleman. One distinction is the same as another. And Dada is even so well thought of in these parts that they have named a cocktail Dada.

But these idyllic days were not to last. Towards the middle of 1921 a certain atmosphere of discontent and quarrelsomeness was beginning to make itself felt. It began with an affair called *La Mise en accusation et jugement de M. Maurice Barrès par DADA*, held on the 13th of May in the hall of the Sociétés Savantes, shortly after which Francis Picabia wrote a series of articles disowning Dada in the popular press. André Breton then announced that his connection with the Dada movement was over. 'The only way for Dada to continue,' he said, 'is for it to cease to exist.' Tzara, on the other hand, had no intention of bringing the movement he had founded to an end. Some Dadaists took Breton's part, others remained faithful to Tzara. Breton conceived the idea of a Congress of Paris for the determination of the modern spirit, and this caused further broils.

In April 1922, a series of Dada tours of Paris was announced. Only one took place, a visit to the church of St Julian le Pauvre. 'The Dadaists passing through Paris,' says the handbill, 'wishing to remedy the incompetence of guides and suspect cicerones, have decided to undertake a series of visits to chosen places, particularly those that have really no reason to exist.' The announcement also tells us: 'Wash your breasts as you wash your gloves'; 'Property is the Luxury of the Poor, Be Dirty'; and adds: 'The piano has very kindly been placed at our disposal by the firm of Gavault.' The name of Benjamin Péret, who had then just come to Paris and was having some success with his *Passager du Transatlantique*, is among those of the Dadaist guides.

In June, a large international Dada exhibition (the last) was held at the Galerie Montaigne [Salon Dada Exposition Internationale, arranged by Tzara]. During the exhibition the Italian Futurists had a matinée at a certain Paris theatre, and the Dadaists attended the performance to manifest their displeasure and scorn; a riot ensued. The owner of the Galerie Montaigne happened to be also the owner of the theatre: he turned the Dadaists out of the gallery and closed down the exhibition. A general reunion at the Closerie de Lilas which followed this incident, consummated the rupture and final ruin of Dada.

Tzara, however, rather foolishly determined to keep the flag flying and published shortly afterwards a bulletin entitled *Coeur à barbe* [The Bearded Heart], to which Picabia replied with another, entitled *La Pomme de pins* [The Pinecone]. In a last desperate attempt to prevent Dada from dying, Tzara then put on a play, also entitled *Coeur à barbe*. A protest meeting, led by Breton, arrived at the theatre for the first performance. The incident that followed is recounted by Breton in the first chapter of *Nadja*:

> M. Tristan Tzara would doubtless prefer that no one knew how on the evening of the *Coeur à barbe* in Paris he 'gave' us, Eluard and me, over to the police, since a spontaneous gesture of that kind is so profoundly significant, and since in the light of this, which surely will be that of history, *25 Poèmes* (the title of one of his books) becomes *25 Lucubrations of a Police-Agent.*

Dada was dead.

CHAPTER THREE

THE PERIOD OF SLEEPING-FITS

Already, in the midst of the tumult of Dada, the seeds of Surrealism were growing. As we have seen, they were perhaps the least Dada elements of the movement (which wasn't a movement), the non-conforming Dadaists, who became Surrealists. So I think we can say that the development from Dadaism to Surrealism was *dialectical.* Dada: negation. Surrealism: negation of negation; a new affirmation, that is. ('A new declaration of the rights of man must be made,' says the cover of the first number of *La Révolution surréaliste*, published in 1924.)

The period that marks the transition from Dadaism to Surrealism (roughly from 1920 to 1923) is often referred to as 'la période des sommeils'. The word *surrealism* had then already been current for some time; it was invented by Guillaume Apollinaire in 1917, as has been recounted in the first chapter.

In 1920 was published the first collection of authentically Surrealist texts, *Les Champs magnétiques* [The Magnetic Fields], written by André Breton and Philippe Soupault in collaboration. André Breton has himself described, in the *Manifeste du surréalisme* [1924], how this first attempt at 'pure psychic automatism' came to be made.

> 'Preoccupied as I still was at that time with Freud,' he says, 'and familiar with his methods of investigation which I had practised occasionally upon the sick during the War' (Breton was originally intended to be a psychiatrist) 'I resolved to obtain from myself what one seeks to obtain from patients, namely a monologue poured out as rapidly as possible, over which the subject's critical faculty has no control – the subject himself throwing reticence to the winds – and which as much as possible represents *spoken thought.* It seemed and still seems to me that the speed of thought is no greater than that of words, and hence does not exceed the flow of either tongue or pen. It was in such circumstances that, together with Philippe Soupault, whom I had told about my first ideas on the subject, I began to cover sheets of paper with writing, feeling a praiseworthy contempt for whatever the literary result might be. Ease of achievement brought about the rest. By the end of the first day of the experiment

we were able to read to one another about fifty pages obtained in this manner and to compare the results we had achieved. The likeness was on the whole striking. There were similar faults of construction, the same hesitant manner and also, in both cases, an illusion of extraordinary verve, much emotion, a considerable assortment of images of a quality such as we should never have been able to obtain in the normal way of writing, a very special sense of the picturesque, and, here and there, a few pieces of out and out buffoonery. The only differences which our two texts presented appeared to me to be due essentially to our respective temperaments, Soupault's being less static than mine, and, if he will allow me to make this slight criticism, to his having scattered about at the top of certain pages – doubtlessly in a spirit of mystification – various words under the guise of titles. I must give him credit, on the other hand, for having always forcibly opposed the least correction of any passage that did not seem to me to be quite the thing. In that he was most certainly right.'

From this experiment to a clear definition of Surrealism it was not far. In an article entitled 'Entrée des médiums' [Enter the Mediums], Breton tells the story of an experience that cropped up on the way and that was undoubtedly of the greatest value to all concerned. This article, published first in *Littérature* (No. 6, second series, November 1922),[1] describes first of all how *Les Champs magnétiques* came to be written and the interest that Breton and his friends had taken, during three years or more, in automatic writing and dreams. The word *surrealism* is for the first time defined. 'This word, which we have not invented, and which we could so easily have left in the vaguest of critical vocabularies, is employed by us with a precise meaning. We have agreed to refer by it to a certain psychic automatism, which more or less corresponds to the dream-state, a state of which it is by this time very difficult to fix the limits.' And here is the second half of the article in full:

A fortnight ago, on his return from holiday, René Crevel told us of the beginning of a 'spiritualist' initiation that he had undergone at the hands of a certain Madame D. . . . This person, having distinguished particular mediumistic qualities in him, had instructed him

[1] Reprinted later in *Les Pas perdus* (Paris: Gallimard, 1924).

in the means of developing them, and so it was, he told us, that under the conditions requisite for these kind of phenomena (darkness and silence in the room, 'chain' of hands about the table) he was enabled to fall rapidly asleep and to pour out words organised into a more or less coherent speech, to which only the awakening put an end. Needless to say that at no time, since the day when we consented to assist in these experiments, have we adopted the spiritualist point of view. As far as I am concerned I formally refuse to admit that any communication whatsoever exists between the living and the dead.

On Monday, September 25th, at nine o'clock in the evening, in the presence of Desnos, Morise and myself, Crevel went into a hypnotic sleep and pronounced a sort of counsel's speech for the defence, which was not noted down. (Declamatory diction, interrupted by sighs, sometimes falling into singing, insistence on certain words, rapid passing over of others, indefinite prolongment of some of the closing phrases, dramatic ending – all in question of a woman accused of killing her husband and whose guilt is contested by the fact that she acted at the request of the latter.) On waking, Crevel had no recollection of his recital. In the following experiment, undertaken in the same conditions, he hardly took part at all. No immediate result. At the end of a quarter of an hour Desnos – who thought himself most unsuited to such manifestations, strengthened as he was in this opinion by the fact that a few days earlier, in my company, he had brought to a standstill the performance of two public magnetisers, MM. Donato and Benevol – let fall his head on to his arms and began to scrape the table convulsively. He woke up of his own accord a few moments later, persuaded that he had not been behaving differently from the rest of us. In order to convince him that he was mistaken we had to notify him separately and in writing of what had taken place.

Crevel having told us that the action of scraping the table might signify a desire to write, it so happened that on the next occasion a pencil was placed in Desnos' hand and a sheet of paper in front of him. In this way, two days later and in similar circumstances, we saw him beneath our very eyes writing, without moving his head, the words: July 14 – 14 July, in addition to plus signs or crosses. It was then that we took to asking him questions:

What do you see?

Death.

He draws a hanged woman at the edge of a road.

Writes: *near the fern are going two* (the rest is lost upon the table).

At this moment I place my hand on his left hand.

Q – *Desnos, this is Breton. Tell us what you see in store for him.*

A – *The Equator* (he draws a circle and a horizontal diameter).

Q – *Should Breton make a journey?*

A – *Yes.*

Q – *Will it be a business journey?*

A – (He signifies no with his hand. Writes): *Nazimova.*

Q – *Will his wife accompany him on this journey?*

A – *? ? ? ?*

Q – *Will he go to look for Nazimova?*

A – *No* (underlined).

Q – *Will he be with Nazimova?*

A – *?*

Q – *What else do you know about Breton? Speak.*

A – *The boat and the snow – there is also the pretty telegraphic tower – on the pretty tower there is a young* (illegible).

I take my hand away. Eluard's replaces it.

Q – *This is Eluard.*

A – *Yes* (drawing).

Q – *What do you know about him?*

A – *Chirico.*

Q – *Is he going to meet Chirico soon?*

A – *The marvellous one with eyes soft as a young baby.*

Q – *What do you see about Eluard?*

A – *He is blue.*

Q – *Why is he blue?*

A – *Because the sky nestles in* (an unfinished, illegible word, the whole sentence is furiously crossed out).

Péret's hand replaces Eluard's.

Q – *What do you know about Péret?*

A – *He will die in a railway-carriage full of people.*

Q – *Does that mean that he will be assassinated?*

A – *Yes.*

Q – *By whom?*

A – (He draws a train with a man falling out of the carriage window) *By an animal.*

Q – *By what animal?*

A – *A blue ribbon, my sweet vagabond.*

Long silence, then: *Speak of her no more, she is going to be born in a few minutes.*

Ernst's hand replaces Péret's.

Q – *It is Ernst who gives you his hand. You know him?*

A – *Who?*
Q – *Max Ernst.*
A – *Yes.*
Q – *Will he live long?*
A – *Fifty-one years.*
Q – *What will he do?*
A – *He will play with the madmen.*
Q – *Will he be happy with these madmen?*
A – *Ask this blue woman.*
Q – *Who is this blue woman?*
A – *THE.*
Q – *What? The?*
A – *Tower.*

Desnos' sleep came to an end. He woke up with a start preceded by violent gestures.

It should be remarked that on the same day, before Desnos' performance, Crevel had passed into a state similar to that of the Monday (another crime story, this time more obscure: *The woman will be naked and it will be the oldest man who will hold the axe*).

During a third attempt made by Eluard, Ernst, Morise, Péret, a young girl who accompanied the latter, Mlle Renée, and myself, Mlle Renée was the first to fall asleep. She soon appeared to be seized by a great agitation and jerked out breathless sentences: *The gulf . . . my father's colourless sweat is drowning me.* (Repetitions. Signs of fright.)

A final attempt gave place at the end of a few minutes to a sudden and very prolonged explosion of laughter from Péret. Was he asleep? It was only with difficulty that we could get any words out of him at all.

What do you see?
Water.
What colour is the water?

Same reply. Tone of conviction.

He rose precipitantly without being asked to, threw himself face down upon the table and pretended to be swimming.

It would be boring to insist longer upon the character of each phenomenon and upon the circumstances in which we saw it produced: Eluard, Ernst, Morise and myself who, in spite of our willingness, did not fall asleep.

⋆ ⋆ ⋆

Surrealism began in 1922 (approximately); from that date until the publication of André Breton's *Manifeste du surréalisme* in 1924 the movement was being determined, clarified, redetermined and discussed. The publications of this period include several numbers of the revue *Littérature*, of which Breton was the editor and which was contributed to by Louis Aragon, Robert Desnos, Paul Eluard, Max Ernst, Benjamin Péret, Francis Picabia (who was shortly to sever connections with Breton and his friends), Roger Vitrac and one or two others; a collection of poems by Breton, *Clair de terre*; *Les Aventures de Télémaque* by Louis Aragon; *Au 125 Boulevard Saint-Germain* by Benjamin Péret (subsequently published in translation in the Surrealist number of *This Quarter*, 1932, and a typical example of Péret's wildly fantastic humour); and two books produced by Paul Eluard and Max Ernst in collaboration: *Répétitions* and *Les Malheurs des immortels*. These two latter works, both published in 1922, must have had a fairly strong influence over the subsequent development of Surrealism; apart from *Les Champs magnétique*, they were the first purely Surrealist books to be published. Eluard had already published three small collections of poems, slight but nevertheless extremely individual and 'pure'. Ernst had just arrived in Paris from Cologne and was arousing much enthusiasm with his paintings and collages. *Les Malheurs des immortels* is an album of fantastic pictures with descriptive comments in prose; *Répétitions* is a collection of poems illustrated by collages. The illustrations, formed of inconsequent fragments cut from Victorian magazines, treatises on anatomy, botany, mechanics, etc., give a most vivid impression of reality. An eye appears as a wooden ball threaded on to a piece of string; in a stable full of horses a queer automatic machine like an armchair is white-washing the wall; in front of a pile of wooden geometrical figures from a drawing-class stands a mediæval warrior to whom a mysterious hand is offering a snake with a head like a razor-blade, and so on.

Here is a translation of a poem by Paul Eluard from *Répétitions*:

THE SHEEP

Close your eyes black face
Close the gardens of the street
Intelligence and hardiness
Ennui and tranquillity
These sad evenings at every moment

The glass and the glass door
Comforting and sensible
And light, the fruit-tree
The flowering tree the fruit-tree
Fly away.

In the early part of 1924 appeared André Breton's *Les Pas perdus*, a collection of essays and articles reprinted from various reviews, which show very clearly the direction of Breton's thought during the period we have been discussing. This was his first book of prose; we find in it all those qualities – clarity, precision, courage, enthusiasm, brilliance of style – which have made him one of the most significant thinkers and writers in contemporary European literature.

In the autumn of 1924 appeared the *Manifeste du surréalisme*, and in December the first number of *La Révolution surréaliste*.

CHAPTER FOUR

THE FIRST MANIFESTO 1924

If today the first *Manifeste du surréalisme* seems to present an in some respects inadequate definition of the aims and methods of the movement, there are nevertheless a number of statements in it that continue to hold good for anything that can properly be called Surrealist. Because it is not a dogma, because its principles have always demanded the maximum amount of freedom in every field, Surrealism has been able to develop to the extent that its external features as they present themselves today are undeniably different from those of over a decade ago, even though its foremost aims have remained unchanged.

It is not in the least surprising that Breton's manifesto should have aroused a considerable sensation. A great deal of animosity and blind opposition, also. André Breton is a man of such strong will, of such steadfast adherence to his beliefs, that he is bound always to have more enemies than friends; many a one-time Surrealist, unable to maintain the standards of disinterestedness and non-conformity that Surrealism demands, has turned upon him with violence and abuse. He has been accused, among other things, of tyrannical authoritativeness, attempted dictatorship, etc. This may or may not to some extent be true; but one thing is certain: that except for André Breton the Surrealist movement could never have existed, for it is as difficult to imagine it without him as it is to imagine psychoanalysis without Freud.

Of all the names cited in the first Manifesto as having 'made the act of Absolute Surrealism', only three remain today. On the other hand, Surrealism in France, in 1935, numbers about thirty adherents. For if Surrealism itself follows a certain logical course of development, most of the Surrealists do not. That is to say that there have been many men, writers and painters, such as Aragon, Desnos, Gerard, Morise, Naville, Soupault, for whom Surrealism has been but a moment in their careers, after which they have passed on, by process of reaction, to journalism, 'socialist realism', pseudo-classicism, and so on. Even to those unsympathetic to Surrealism, such conduct must appear as a sign of fundamental weakness of character. One could fill the rest of this book with accounts of the personal quarrels among the Surrealists occasioned by such cases of weakness and reaction, but not wishing to do that let us return to a consideration of the first Manifesto.

Man's imagination should be free, yet everywhere is in chains, is the theme of the opening pages. Chains of preconception, be it understood. 'To reduce the imagination to slavery,' says the author, 'even when that slavery goes by the gross name of happiness, is to strip one's self of every remnant of the supreme justice that is to be found at the bottom of each one of us.' He goes on to discuss the advantages of madness, a form of freedom that is also, unfortunately, a tyranny, because one cannot control it at will. He then opens his famous attack on rationalism:

> We still live under the reign of logic; that, as you will well understand, is what I want to come to. But the methods of logic are applied nowadays only to the resolution of problems of secondary interest. The absolute rationalism which is still the fashion does not permit consideration of any facts but those strictly relevant to our experience. Logical ends, on the other hand, escape us. Needless to say that even experience has had limits assigned to it. It revolves in a cage from which it becomes more and more difficult to release it. Even experience is dependent on immediate utility, and common sense is its keeper. Under colour of civilisation, under pretext of progress, all that rightly or wrongly may be regarded as fantasy or superstition has been banished from the mind, all uncustomary searching after truth has been proscribed. It is only what must seem sheer luck that there has recently been brought to light an aspect of mental life – to my belief by far the most important – with which it was supposed that we no longer had any concern. All credit for these discoveries must go to Freud. Based on these discoveries a current of opinion is forming that will enable the explorer of the human mind to extend his investigations, justified as he will be in taking into account more than mere summary realities. The imagination is perhaps on the point of reclaiming its rights. If the depths of our mind harbour strange forces capable of increasing those of the surface, or of successfully contending with them, then it is all in our interest to canalise them, to canalise them first in order to submit them later, if necessary, to the control of reason. The analysts themselves have nothing to lose by such a proceeding. But it should be observed that there are no means designed *a priori* for the bringing about of such an enterprise, that until the coming of the new

order it might just as well be considered to be the affair of poets and scientists, and that its success will not depend on the more or less capricious means that will be employed.

Having amplified this theme and examined at closer range the 'strange forces' harboured by our minds and that are manifested in 'madness, dream, the absurd, the incoherent, the hyperbolic and everything that is opposed to the summary appearance of the real', in the words of Georges Hugnet, Breton goes on to say: 'One should take the trouble to *practise* poetry.' This is where those who imagine Surrealism to be simply an experimental extension of literature and art are confounded. The most vital feature of Surrealism is its exclusive interest in that point at which literature and art give place to real life, that point at which the imagination seeks to express itself in a more concrete form than words or plastic images. Hence the Surrealists' frequent reference to this phrase of Lautréamont's: 'Poetry should be made by all. Not one.'

After an account of certain early Surrealist experiments, part of which I have already quoted, Breton makes 'once and for all' the following definition, which is by no means so well known in England that I need not quote it here:

> SURREALISM, n. Pure psychic automatism, by which it is intended to express, verbally, in writing, or by other means, the real process of thought. Thought's dictation, in the absence of all control exercised by the reason and outside all aesthetic or moral preoccupations.
>
> ENCYCL. *Philos.* Surrealism rests in the belief in the superior reality of certain forms of association neglected heretofore; in the omnipotence of the dream and in the disinterested play of thought. It tends definitely to do away with all other psychic mechanisms and to substitute itself for them in the solution of the principal problems of life.

There you have the essentials of Surrealism in a few words. A number of supplementary definitions could be added today[1] (as indeed they have been in André Breton's pamphlet *Qu'est-ce que le surréalisme?* [What is Surrealism?], published in Belgium in 1934), but the above remains pretty well as valid as when it was first written.

[1] Notably concerning the experimental paranoia of Salvador Dalí. See page 36.

The Manifesto continues with a list of writers, philosophers and others, past and present, who may in one way or another be considered as Surrealists. The reader will find this list of names reproduced on the flap of the wrapper of the present book.* Breton has been careful to note, however, that

> They were not always Surrealists, in the sense that one can disentangle in each of them a number of preconceived notions to which – very naively! – they clung. And they clung to them so because they had not heard the *surrealist voice*, the voice that exhorts on the eve of death and in the roaring storm, and because they were unwilling to dedicate themselves to the task of no more than orchestrating the score replete with marvellous things. They were proud instruments; hence the sounds they produced were not always harmonious sounds.
>
> We, on the contrary, who have not given ourselves to processes of filtering, who through the medium of our work have been content to be the silent receptacle of many echoes, modest *registering machines* that are not hypnotised by the pattern that they trace, we are perhaps yet serving a much nobler cause. So we honestly give back the talent lent to us. You may talk of the 'talent' of this yard of platinum, of this mirror, of this door and of this sky, if you wish.
>
> We have no talents, asks *Philippe Soupault*: 'The anatomical manufactories and the cheap abodes shall destroy the highest towns.'
>
> *Roger Vitrac*:
> 'Scarcely had I invoked the marble-admiral than the latter turned on his heel like a horse that shies at the Pole star and marked out on the surface of his cocked-hat a region where I was to spend my life.'
>
> *Paul Eluard*:
> 'It is a well-known story that I tell, a celebrated poem that I re-read: I am leaning against a wall, with verdant ears and calcinated lips.'
>
> *Max Morise*:
> 'The cave-bear and the lout his companion, the *vol-au-vent* and the wind his valet, the Lord High Chancellor and his wife, the sparrow-scarer and the old fellow his compère, the test-tube and her daughter the needle, the cannibal and his brother the carnival,

---

* See Appendix 2, page 122.

the crossing-sweeper and his monocle, the Mississippi and its little dog, the coral and its milk-can, the Miracle and its dear God have nothing left to do than to disappear from the surface of the sea.'

Joseph Delteil:
'Alas! I am a believer in the virtue of birds. And it only needs a feather to make me die of laughing.'

Louis Aragon:
'During an interruption of the party, while the players were joining around a bowl of flaming punch, I asked the tree whether it always wore its red ribbon.

'And myself, who have been unable to stop writing the bewildered and serpentine lies of this preface.

'Ask Robert Desnos, the one of us who has perhaps got nearer to Surrealist truth than anyone, and who, in certain recent works and throughout many experiments to which he has given himself, has fully justified the hope I place in Surrealism and allows me to expect much from it. Desnos today *speaks* surrealistically at will.'[2]

That is a long enough quotation; and to tell the truth I should have liked to translate the entire Manifesto from beginning to end; but must be content with simply making a short résumé of its concluding sections.

The passage I have just quoted is followed by a number of 'recipes' for Surrealist writing, talking, etc., in the manner of Raymond Lulle; these should not be taken too seriously. The discussion of language that follows this section is worthy of more attention. 'Language has been given to man that he may make a Surrealist use of it.' In conversation, for instance, when one person replies quite irrespective of what the other has said. In unpremeditated images, such as Reverdy's, 'The day was folded like a white cloth.' All this is in order to bring about the fusion of two mutually distant realities. (The most celebrated example of such a fusion is, of course, the 'chance meeting, on a dissecting-table, of a sewing-machine and an umbrella', of Lautréamont, an image which brings about the union of two mutually distant realities upon a plane equally unrelated to either of them.)

---

[2] It should be noted that Robert Desnos very soon lost this faculty. He has had no connection with the Surrealist movement for many years.

In Surrealism one relives the best of childhood; it should be possible to establish certain rules concerning Surrealism; Surrealist poems can be composed from random newspaper-cuttings ('collage' poems); Surrealism possesses its devotee like the voice of the ancient oracles: such are the chief remaining points of the Manifesto, which ends:

> Surrealism, as I envisage it, displays our complete *non-conformity* so clearly that there can be no question of claiming it as a witness when the real world comes up for trial. On the contrary, it can but testify to the complete state of distraction to which we hope to attain here below. Kant distracted by women, Pasteur distracted by 'grapes', Curie distracted by traffic, are profoundly symptomatic in this respect. The world is only very relatively proportionate to thought and incidents of this kind are only the most striking episodes of a war of independence in which I glory in taking part. Surrealism is the 'invisible ray' that shall enable us one day to overcome our enemies. 'You tremble no more, carcase.' This summer the roses are blue; the wood is made of glass. The earth wrapped in its foliage makes as little effect on me as a ghost. Living and ceasing to live are imaginary solutions. Existence is elsewhere.[3]

★ ★ ★

The Surrealists made their first public protest in October 1924, on the occasion of the death of Anatole France. On the day of his funeral they published and distributed in Paris a pamphlet entitled simply: *A Corpse.* 'It should be a fête-day on which cunning, traditionalism, patriotism, opportunism, scepticism, realism and heartlessness are buried!' wrote Breton in this joint declaration of disgust.

La Révolution surréaliste made its first appearance two months later, under the direction of Benjamin Péret and Pierre Naville. (It should be mentioned that a 'Central Bureau of Surrealist Research' had been open in Paris since the previous October.) The opening number of this first Surrealist review contained dreams, automatic texts and a number of illustrations by de Chirico, Max Ernst, André Masson, Picasso and Man Ray. On one page there is a photo of the Nice carnival and on another a 'still' from a Buster Keaton film, and an entire

---

[3] In the same volume as the Manifesto were published thirty-two Surrealist texts, under the title *Soluble Fish.*

page is devoted to photographs of the Surrealists, with Germaine Berton, the then famous anarchist, in their midst. The most provocative feature is the announcement in large type of an enquête: IS SUICIDE A SOLUTION? At the foot of every other page there are press cuttings relative to suicide.

The second number, which appeared in January 1925, has a photo of a scarecrow on the cover, with the caption: 'French art at the beginning of the twentieth century.' Numerous answers to the suicide enquiry, most of them stupid, are printed. At the end, the question is asked again; it is one that none but the dead could answer. The most important features of this number were an article by Breton, 'The Last Strike', and a declaration headed: 'OPEN THE PRISONS, DISBAND THE ARMY.' A growing political conscience, confused as yet, is recognisable in Breton's article, in which he says: 'I believe with all truly free men that the Revolution, even with its abuses, remains the highest and most moving expression that can be given to that love of Good in which the universal will and individual wills are united'; and also, though quite negatively, in an article by Louis Aragon, today a strictly orthodox member of the Communist Party, in which he refers to the Russian Revolution as a 'vague ministerial crisis', and defends himself for having written of 'doddering Moscow'.

Number three of *La Révolution surréaliste* contrived to be even more sensational than its predecessors. Here are the headings of some of the pages: 'Letter to the Rectors of the Universities of Europe'; 'Address to the Pope'; 'Address to the Dalai-Lama'; 'Letter to the Buddhist Schools'; 'Letter to the Directors of Lunatic Asylums'. There are also automatic texts and drawings, dreams, poems and photographs as before.

The fourth number, May 1925, opens with an article by Breton entitled: 'Why I have taken over the Editorship of *The Surrealist Revolution*'. One of the reasons for the change was that Pierre Naville, the previous editor, had stated that there could be no such thing as Surrealist painting. Breton contradicted this by publishing the first instalment of his long study, 'Surrealism and Painting', subsequently published in book form. We shall refer to this later. It should be remarked that the first collective exhibition of Surrealist painting took place in November of the same year [at the Galerie Pierre, Paris].

In July, a fresh scandal. Paul Claudel, the well-known Catholic and reactionary writer, had insulted Dadaism and Surrealism in an interview published in the paper *Comœdia*. 'Neither Dadaism nor Surrealism,' he said, 'have anything but a single meaning: pederastic.' There immediately followed the famous 'Open Letter to M. Paul Claudel, Ambassador of France to Japan', printed on a single sheet of bright red paper and distributed widely among the general public. 'Write, pray and drivel,' said the twenty-eight signatories of this letter; 'we claim the dishonour of having called you once and for all a prig and a scoundrel.'

The same month marked the return to Paris of an old and forgotten poet whom the Surrealists much admired, Saint-Pol-Roux [Pierre-Paul Roux], known as the Magnificent. A banquet was given in his honour at the Closerie de Lilas, and once more this café was the scene of violence and disorder, for a number of persons of high importance in the literary world had been invited, and when they sat down to table they each found a copy of the letter to Claudel beneath their napkins. The anti-patriotic and subversive after-dinner speeches of the Surrealists caused these literary gentlemen to react in the most violent manner. A fight ensued and the interrupted dessert gave place to intervention by the police.

* * *

The appearance of the fifth number of *La Révolution surréaliste*, a month or so after the events described above, marks the complete adherence of the Surrealists to Communism. 'The Revolution Now and Ever' is the title of the manifesto presented with this number. It is a declaration against patriotism, against France and against the imperialist war in Morocco which was at that time occupying national attention. It was signed by all the Surrealists and also by a number of other revolutionary writers connected with the reviews *Clarté, Correspondance* and *Philosophies*. Since the appearance of this manifesto the development of Surrealism has been an entirely dialectical one. The principles of Marxism have given the movement a unity and a purpose that to a large extent were lacking until then. Without the philosophy of dialectical materialism behind it, Surrealism could hardly have existed until today and be still a living force.

If the period from the end of 1925 till the *Second Manifeste du surréalisme* at the end of 1929 was one of difficulties with the Communist

Party on the one hand (the Communists have always treated Breton and the Surrealists with a quite unjustifiable suspicion and mistrust), and of personal weaknesses on the other, it was also one of growing confidence and power for Surrealism; it saw the appearance of works such as André Breton's *Nadja*, Paul Eluard's *Capitale de la douleur, Les Dessous d'une vie, L'Amour la poésie*, Benjamin Péret's *Dormir, dormir dans les pierres, Le Grand Jeu, . . . Et les Seins mouraient*, René Crevel's *L'Esprit contre la raison, Babylone* and *Etes-vous fous?*, Louis Aragon's *Paysan de Paris*, Robert Desnos' *La Liberté ou l'amour*, and Max Ernst's 'collage' novel, *La Femme 100 Têtes* – works in which the pure spirit of revolt reached a height of expression almost never before equalled; it saw numerous exhibitions of paintings by artists such as Arp, de Chirico, Ernst, Miró, Picasso, Man Ray and Yves Tanguy.

The period of preliminary experiment and research that followed the breakdown of Dada was at last bearing fruit. The works I have mentioned naturally I cannot go into in full detail here, but I think I should outline a few of the most important.

The *Nadja* of André Breton is a history of facts. It is an account of an episode in Breton's life during which he made the acquaintance of an extraordinary woman possessed of outstanding Surrealist faculties. It is a disturbing book and cannot but give place in the reader's mind to a profound doubt concerning the validity of the normal, everyday world in which we live. There is a pathetic side to the story, for Nadja in the end went mad. The book closes with a very justifiable criticism of lunatic asylums and their officials, which caused Breton to be vigorously attacked in the medical press. He replied to these attacks in an article called 'The Treatment of Mental Disease and Surrealism', in which he said:

> We consider it due to our honour to be the first to call attention to this danger, to make a stand against this unbearable, and increasing, abuse of power by people whom we are inclined to look upon as being not so much doctors as gaolers and indeed as purveyors of penal settlements and scaffolds. . . . We cannot urge them too strongly, even if some of them are doomed to be struck down accidentally by the blows of those whom they seek arbitrarily to control, to have the decency to shut up.

Le Surréalisme et le peinture [Surrealism and Painting] is a brilliant and detailed study of that manifestation of Surrealism which is as yet the best known side of it in England and America. I need hardly remind the reader of the immense importance in modern art of such painters as Picasso, whom I should not hesitate to call pre-eminently a Surrealist painter; de Chirico, painter of those great deserted towns which we all seem to remember having visited in one or other of our major dreams;[4] Max Ernst, with his *Histoire Naturelle*, produced by rubbing paper with charcoal across the uneven surfaces of wood and stone, his mythology of birds and suns and infernal demi-gods, his shell-flowers and flower-birds, the very flora and fauna of dream, and his astonishing books of 'collage' pictures, in which the poetry of nightmare is given enduring form;[5] Arp, who reveals a world of freshness, humour and great simplicity in bas-reliefs of plaster and wood; Miró, whose painting is of a type as old as art itself, spontaneous, vivid and full of verve, whose Ballet *Jeux d'Enfants* 'has had in England a success among thousands who did not suspect that what was before them to enjoy had been invented by a "modern" artist and even by a "mad" Surrealist';[6] Tanguy, creator of the most tragic landscapes that the eye has never seen; and Man Ray, who has raised photography to all the dignity of painting and has trapped the world of shadows with his lens. If we find no mention of the work of Salvador Dalí in this book of Breton's, which appeared in 1928, it is

---

[4] *The World of de Chirico.* We cannot tell the hour, for these elongated shadows across the square are not those of sundials; beneath the arches of the colonnades they are mystery. Against the infinity of the horizon a train moves towards Nowhere, releasing phantom plumes of smoke.

Beyond the immobile equestrian statue which has stood at the edge of the square for so long that one has forgotten whom it commemorates, the sea lies waiting for the hour when it shall rise to overwhelm this dead and empty city. Roman soldiers wander and terrific horses gallop over the sands.

We enter the colonnade and find our way into a white-washed room. Here there are plaster casts of heads of a type of beauty now extinct, there are gloves, T-squares, cornices, laths, picture-frames, handles of violins, biscuits and strangely-marked wands.

Coming towards us from the doorway with slow, agonising movements is a menacing and abnormally tall figure, swathed, its head featureless as an egg, with bricks, scaffoldings, models of buildings and little arches tumbling from its dreadful breast. Its arm creaks as it raises its rubber hand to point at us, meaninglessly. . . .

[5] *La Femme 100 Têtes* (1929), *Rêve d'une petite fille qui voulut entrer au Carmel* (1930), *Une Semaine de bonté* (1934).

[6] Geoffrey Grigson, in *The Arts To-day* (London: Bodley Head, 1935).

because the first exhibition of Dalí's paintings did not take place until November 1929; they will be referred to later.[7]

The poems of Paul Eluard are pure crystallisations of tenderness and simplicity, of passion and revolt. Not only does he represent by far the highest achievement of Surrealist poetry, he is one of the most considerable French poets living, a direct descendant of Baudelaire. I have already spoken of his *Répétitions* in the previous chapter. *Capitale de la douleur* and *L'Amour la poésie* represent a further step towards the complete confidence and power of his most recent poems. *Les Dessous d'une vie, ou La Pyramide humaine* is a collection of dreams, Surrealist texts and poems. 'Uselessness of poetry,' says the preface to this last volume: 'the perceptible world is excluded from Surrealist texts and the most sublime cold light shines on the heights where the mind enjoys such liberty as it would never dream of verifying.'

The importance of Louis Aragon to Surrealism during the time when he belonged to the movement (we shall have occasion to speak of his 'conversion' to the Communist Party later on) should not be underestimated. *Le Paysan de Paris* (1926) is the work in which he gave fullest play to his brilliant imagination. It is a study of the Surrealist aspect of the old Passage de l'Opéra in Paris, during its last days before it was pulled down to make way for the Boulevard Haussman.

'Our contributor Benjamin Péret insulting a priest', is the title of one of the photographs published in *La Révolution surréaliste*. It gives a graphic idea of the character of Péret's poems and stories, their brutal, bitter, crazy humour. His hatred of the existing order is evident even in his quietest fantasies. In addition to the collections of his work that I have mentioned, he published in 1925, in collaboration with Paul Eluard, a series of '152 Proverbs adapted to the contemporary taste', from which I extract the following: 'The further it is from the urn, the longer the beard.' – 'Three dates in a flute.' – 'Beat your mother while she's young.' – 'Cold meat puts out no fire.' – 'Skin that peels goes to heaven.' – 'He who sows fingernails reaps a

[7] In his first Manifesto Breton wrote: 'I could say as much (that they were Surrealist) for certain painters, to mention only Uccello of ancient times. Of the modern period Seurat, Gustave Moreau, Matisse (in "Music" for example), Derain, Picasso (by far the purest), Braque, Duchamp, Picabia, de Chirico (so long admirable), Klee, Man Ray, Max Ernst, and, so close to us, André Masson.'

torch.' – 'There is always a skeleton in the buffet.' – 'All that fattens is not soft.' – 'Faithful as a boneless cat.' – 'A corset in July is worth a horde of rats.' – 'I came, I sat down, I went away.' (These proverbs remind me of a Surrealist game called 'The Exquisite Corpse', after one of the sentences produced while playing it. You sit four or five about a table and pass round a sheet of paper, each one writing in turn, the first an adjective, the second a noun, the third a verb, the fourth an adjective, the fifth a noun. In this way complete sentences are obtained, such as: 'The winged vapour seduces the locked bird.' – 'The Senegal oyster shall eat the tri-coloured bread.' – 'The headless stars circle round the folded and unfolded cinema-programme.' – 'The anaemic little girl makes the polished mannequins blush.' – Another version of the game is known to children as 'Heads, Bodies and Legs'. Yet another Surrealist game consists of questions and answers, without the interrogated party knowing what he is being asked, as: Q. 'What is butter?' – A. 'It is the circle of the mirror, the reflection of a circle.' – Q. 'What is the sun?' – A. 'A polar region, very cold in summer and very hot in winter.')

Finally I must mention the work of René Crevel, whose recent tragic death was a great loss to the Surrealist movement. His persistent attacks on modern society and the antiquated systems of thought that just manage to hold it together were particularly distinguished by great vigour, sincerity and brilliance of style. 'A novel by Crevel is always more or less a dream, but a dream that allows one to go beyond realism into the deeper existence of things,' said a French critic of *Etes-vous fous?* There is a good translation by Kay Boyle of a story of his from *Babylone*, 'Mr Knife and Miss Fork', in Number 18 of the American review *transition*; it is a study of the dream-life of a little girl in an unhappy household.

(The poems of René Char should be mentioned here also, as his *Arsenal* first appeared in 1929. They can best be likened to pieces of clear crystal in which the most vivid irrational images are perpetuated, like snowstorms in paperweights.)

From all this it should be clear that Surrealism is by no means simply a recipe, or 'specific method of creation'. Rather it is a starting-point for works of the most striking diversity, capable of almost infinite variation and development.

* * *

The uneasy relationship between Surrealism and the Communist Party is revealed in such works as Pierre Naville's *La Révolution et les intellectuels*, André Breton's *Légitime Défense*, and particularly in the declaration to the Communists, *Au Grand Jour*, all published in 1927. Again and again the Surrealists have been forced to point out that a consciousness of the class-struggle does not necessarily express itself in terms of 'socialist realism', that the need for writing of the propaganda type does not in itself condemn research along other lines and that Communism has nothing to gain by suppressing the liberty of thought and expression of declared revolutionaries united in their hatred of the capitalist bourgeoisie and taking every opportunity to make clear their political attitude and their faith in dialectical-materialism. (They have recently been driven openly to declare their defiance of the Communist Party, which at present seems to be showing itself more than ever bent on disproving Lenin's contention that a party manifests its strength by being able to support division in its ranks.) A French critic once displayed a considerable sense of proportion by observing that 'the whole activity of the Surrealists cannot be reduced to a simple automatism. They use writing in quite a voluntary fashion, contradictory to the feeling that they have for this automatism, and for ends that cannot be gone into here. One can state quite simply that their actions and their painting belong to that vast enterprise of re-creating the universe to which both Lautrémont and Lenin gave themselves entirely.'

Meanwhile, *La Révolution surréaliste* continued to appear. Number 9-10, October 1927, contains a sensational document headed (in English) 'HANDS OFF LOVE'. This is a full statement of the Surrealist attitude towards sexual morality, occasioned by the Chaplin divorce case. It was first published in the review *transition*, Number 6, but apparently the Surrealists were dissatisfied with the manner of its presentation there and so reprinted the original French text in their own periodical. Number 11 made its appearance in March 1928, and is chiefly remarkable for the 'Researches on Sexuality' that it contains. As I remarked at the beginning of this chapter, the Surrealists have always demanded the maximum amount of liberty in every field, and the field of sexuality is in no way an exception to this. Their attitude towards sex is almost identical with that of the Marquis de Sade or William Blake. The same number contains an article by Breton and Aragon marking the fiftieth anniversary of hysteria (defined by Charcot at Salpetrière in 1878).

A year and nine months elapsed between the appearance of the 11th and the 12th and last number of *La Révolution surréaliste*. During this time the only sign of concerted Surrealist activity was the special number of the Belgian review *Variétés* devoted to 'Surrealism in 1929' (June). The reason for this silence is to be found in the fact that this was a period of grave internal crisis for Surrealism. A long series of petty bickerings, reactions and betrayals was coming to a head, to be finally dealt with by André Breton in his *Second Manifeste du surréalisme*, published in the final number of *La Révolution surréaliste*, December 1929.

CHAPTER FIVE

THE SECOND MANIFESTO 1929

It is not my intention to go into in full detail here of the *Second Manifeste du surréalisme* (a substantial part of which has already been translated in the Surrealist number of *This Quarter*), even though it is in many ways more important than the first. The function it performed was that of restating the Surrealist programme in the light of five years' active experience, and of breaking away from certain former collaborators who had shown themselves incapable of maintaining the standards required of them.

It was no doubt unfortunate for Surrealism that MM. Artaud, Carrive, Delteil, Gerard, Limbour, Masson, Soupault and Vitrac should have turned to journalism, commercialism and calumnious disloyalty; that MM. Baron and Naville should have found it more paying to flirt with *vulgar-marxismus*; that MM. Desnos and Ribemont-Dessaignes should have been unable to resist the temptation to enter the 'literary world' with its vulgar prospects of 'success'. But it was possible to dispense with their services without the Surrealist movement being in any way seriously disabled by their loss. Breton was merciless, no doubt, and his vigorous denunciation of those who had once regarded him as their friend was unhesitatingly brought up against him by his enemies, who had not, perhaps, realised that his attachment to the original purity of Surrealism was so profound that nothing, certainly not fear of intolerance, would prevent him from defending it.

Since I have not the space at my disposal to translate here the entire Manifesto, a large part of which is devoted to dealing with the cases of the various former Surrealists mentioned above, I will content myself with quoting its opening and its conclusion.

> Whatever may have been the controversial issues raised by former or present followers of Surrealism, all will admit that the drift of Surrealism has always and chiefly been towards a general and emphatic *crisis in consciousness* and it is only when this is happening or is shown to be impossible that the success or historic eclipse of the movement will be decided.

Intellectually it was and still is a question of exposing by every available means, and to learn at all price to identify, the factitious nature of the conflicts hypocritically calculated to hinder the setting on foot of any unusual agitation to give mankind were it only a faint understanding of its latent possibilities and to inspire it to free itself from its fetters by all the means available. The horror of death, the pantomime of the beyond, the total breakdown of the most beautiful intellect in dream, the towers of Babel, the mirror of inconstancies, the insuperable silver-splashed wall of the brain, all these startling images of human catastrophes are perhaps nothing but images after all.

There is a hint in all this of a belief that there exists a certain spiritual plane on which life and death, the real and the imaginary, the past and the future, the communicable and the incommunicable, the high and the low, are not conceived of as opposites. It would therefore be vain to attribute to Surrealism any other motive than the hope to determine that plane, as it would be absurd to ascribe to it a purely destructive or constructive character: the point at issue being precisely this, that construction and destruction should no longer be flaunted against one another. It becomes clear also that Surrealism is not at all interested in taking into account what passes alongside it under the guise of art and is in fact anti-art, philosophy or anti-philosophy, all, in a word, that has not for its ultimate end the conversion of the being into a jewel, internal and unseeing, with a soul that is neither of ice nor of fire. What, indeed, do they expect of Surrealism, who are still anxious about the position they may occupy *in the world*? On that mental plane from which one may for oneself alone embark on the perilous, but, we think, supreme exploit, on that plane the footfalls of those who come or go are no longer of any importance, because their echo will be repeated in a land in which, by delimitation, Surrealism possesses no listening ear. It is not desirable that Surrealism should be dependent on the whim of this or that person. If it declares itself capable of ransoming thought to a serfdom more and more task-driven, to bring it back to the path of complete understanding, to restore it to its pristine purity, it is indeed no more than right that it should be judged only by what it has done and by what it has still to accomplish in the fulfilment of its promise.

* * *

Surrealism is less ready than ever to accept departures from this and to content itself with what both this set of persons and that are ready to devote to it in between a couple of little betrayals which they think justified by the obscure and revolting pretext that one must live. We will not put up with this charity of the 'talents'. It seems to us that what we are asking for is something involving either a wholehearted assent or a wholehearted refusal, and that there must be no mere pouring out of empty words nor mere profession of fanciful hopes. Is a man ready to risk everything so that at the very bottom of the crucible into which we propose throwing our poor abilities, what remains of our reputation and our doubts, all jumbled up with the jolly 'sensible' glassware, the radical notion of impotence and the absurdity of our supposed duties, he may have the joy of catching a glimpse of *the light which will cease to flicker*?

We maintain that the only chance of success for the Surrealist operation lies in its being performed under conditions of moral asepsis, and the idea of this asepsis is still one that few men will entertain. Yet otherwise there can be no arresting of that cancer of the mind which consists in thinking far too sadly that certain things 'are' when others, which might so well be, 'are not'. We have contended that the things which are and the things which might so well be should be fused, or thoroughly intercept each other, at the limits. What has to be done is not to be content with that, but *to be unable to do less than tend desperately towards those limits.*

A man who wrongly allows himself to be put off by a few monstrous historical failures, is still free to *believe* in his freedom. He is his own master, despite the old clouds which pass and his blind powers which stumble. Has he not a sense of brief and stolen beauty and of accessible, enduring and stealable beauty? That key of love which the poet claimed to have found, he too, if only he takes the trouble to look, he too has it. It depends solely on him whether he shall rise above the fleeting feeling of living dangerously and of dying. Let him despise all prohibitions and let him make use of that avenging weapon, the *idea*, against the beastliness of all beings and all things, and let him on the day when he is defeated – but he will be defeated only *if the world is the world* – let him treat the firing of the pathetic rifles as a volley of salute.[1]

Before passing on it should be said that between these two passages are to be found: a reconsideration of the original Surrealist method of

[1] Translation by Edward W. Titus, from *This Quarter*, Vol. 5, No. 1 (September 1932).

automatism, a clear definition of the strict moral attitude of Surrealism, and a restatement of the Surrealists' faith in dialectical materialism: ('How allow that the dialectical method is only to be applied validly to solving social problems? It is the whole of Surrealism's ambition to supply this method with nowise conflicting possibilities of application in the most immediate conscious domain. I really cannot see, *pace* a few muddle-headed revolutionaries, why we should abstain from taking up the problems of love, of dreaming, of madness, of art, of religion, so long as we consider these problems from the same angle as they, and we too, consider Revolution.') The *Second Manifeste* is clearly an event of considerable importance in the history of Surrealism and should be studied in its entirety by anyone particularly interested in the movement.

A month or so after the first appearance of the Manifesto, those whom it had excluded from the group retaliated with a pamphlet entitled: *A Corpse* (after the famous Anatole France pamphlet), on the cover of which was to be found a faked photograph of André Breton crowned with thorns, and which contained nothing of any interest, only a series of remarkably violent insults; the signatories made no attempt to disprove the accusations that Breton had brought against them.

The twelfth and last number of *La Révolution surréaliste* (shortly to be replaced by *Le Surréalisme au service de la révolution*) contained many other remark-worthy features besides the *Second Manifeste*. – Tristan Tzara, his quarrel with Breton mended after a period of seven years, during which, after the liquidation of Dada, he had been publishing poems that were fully in accord with the principles of Surrealism (*Mouchoir de nuages*, 1925; *Indicateur des chemins de cœur*, 1928; *De Nos Oiseaux*, 1929), was represented in this number by a long fragment from his then most recent poem, *L'Homme approximatif* (a translation of which is to be found on pages 114–18 of the present volume[2]). I am inclined to regard this as one of the finest achievements of Surrealist poetry; certainly it is one of the most remarkable French poems written since the War. Considering its great length, the perpetual flow of absolutely new and very striking images is an almost unparalleled feat in itself; the culminating effect is indeed that of the primitive emotional and constructive power that is concealed in the depths of the essential, integral being of man.

---

[2] See also: *This Quarter* and *transition*, No. 19-20.

Examples of the painting of Salvador Dalí, whose first exhibition had taken place the previous month, were reproduced for the first time in this number of *La Révolution surréaliste*. The entrance of this figure into Surrealist activity was in itself enough to compensate for the loss of those with whom connections had just been severed. Another important feature consisted of the scenario of the film, *Un Chien andalou*, which had caused much scandal and sensation at its first showings at the Studio 28 cinema during the autumn of 1929. With the exception of an experimental film by Man Ray, *L'Etoile de mer* (1928), for which Robert Desnos wrote the script, and *La Perle* (1929), a film by Georges Hugnet, who at that time had no connection with the Surrealist movement, *Un Chien andalou*, by Salvador Dalí and Luis Buñuel, was the first Surrealist film to be produced. It is a grotesque and terrifying film, liable to cause hysteria among audiences from whom Karloff could not raise the least shiver. Sample shot:

> The following pass across the screen: first, a cork, then a melon, then two teachers from a church school, and finally two magnificent grand pianos. The pianos are filled with the carcasses of donkeys, their legs, tails, hind-quarters and excrement sticking out of the piano-cases. As one piano passes across the screen, a huge donkey's head is seen resting on its keyboard.

Containing, among other items, an article which tells us 'How to Deal with Priests', a series of poems by Benjamin Péret, an article by the Belgian painter René Magritte concerning the relation between words and visual images, an article by a doctor on the unconscious motives of suicide, a series of notes on the nature of poetry by Breton and Eluard, and an article by Aragon entitled 'Introduction to 1930', the review closes with a number of answers to the enquiry: *What sort of hope do you place in love?*

* * *

During the spring of 1930, at Avignon, where they were on holiday together, André Breton, René Char and Paul Eluard collaborated in an experiment to which they gave the name of *Ralentir travaux*. This was a collection of poems, not poems by three different people but poems in each of which all three had taken a hand. The results were on the whole surprisingly good. There should be no need to point out the extreme anti-individualist nature of such an experiment.

On their return to Paris, the first number of *Le Surréalisme au service de la révolution* was produced, a marked improvement, one can unhesitatingly say, on its predecessor. It opens with a telegram received by the Surrealists from the International Bureau of Revolutionary Literature, Moscow:

> 'Kindly reply to the following question: What will be your position if Imperialism declares war on the Soviets?' To which the reply: 'Comrades, if Imperialism declares war on the Soviets our position will conform to the directions of the Third International, position of the Communist Party of France.
>
> 'If you can think of better employment for our faculties in such a case we are at your disposal for precise mission in so much as intellectuals. To submit suggestions to you would be to presume upon our rôle and circumstances.
>
> 'In the present situation of non-armed conflict we believe it useless to wait to put at the service of the revolution the means that are particularly ours.'

Still looked upon only with suspicion by the Communist Party, it was reassuring to the Surrealists to know that at least their existence was acknowledged by Moscow.

A declaration of solidarity with André Breton is printed on another page, signed by Maxime Alexandre, Aragon, Joë Bousquet, Luis Buñuel, René Char, René Crevel, Salvador Dalí, Paul Eluard, Max Ernst, Marcel Fourrier, Camille Goemans, Georges Malkine, Paul Nougé, Benjamin Péret, Francis Ponge, Marco Ristitch, Georges Sadoul, Yves Tanguy, André Thirion, Tristan Tzara and Albert Valentin.

Perhaps the most important feature of the first number of this review is André Breton's article on the suicide of the Soviet poet, Mayakovsky, one of the few Russian poets since the Revolution to attempt to widen the rather narrow limits of 'proletarian literature'. 'More than ever,' wrote Breton, 'now that Mayakovsky is dead, we refuse to register the weakening of the spiritual and moral position that he took up. We deny, and shall continue to do so, the possibility of a poetry or of an art susceptible of accommodating itself to extremist simplification – à la Barbusse – of ways of thinking and feeling. We have yet to be shown a "proletarian" work of art. The enthusiastic life of the struggling proletariat, the stupifying and shattering life of the mind a prey to its own beasts, for our part it would be too vain to wish to take part in only one of these two distinct dramas. Expect no concession from us in this domain.'

The Surrealists had a great admiration for Mayakovsky, a truly revolutionary poet but one who made no compromise between his conception of poetry and the superficial idea of propaganda that he found himself up against. A stupid article published in *Les Nouvelles Littéraires* shortly after Mayakovsky's death provoked Louis Aragon to visit its author and teach him a painful lesson.

In the same number of this review are to be found photographs from the second film of Salvador Dalí and Luis Buñuel, *L'Age d'or*, which when shown at the Studio 28 created an even greater scandal than *Un Chien andalou*: repeated riots caused the police to close it down at the end of a week. 'My general idea in writing with Buñuel the scenario of *The Golden Age*,' wrote Dalí in the manifesto programme, 'has been to present the straight and pure line of "conduct" of a man who pursues love in face of ignoble humanitarian, patriotic ideals and other miserable mechanisms of reality.' The film, which opens with an allegory of the founding of Rome and closes with an incident from the Marquis de Sade's *120 Jours en Sodome*, tells the story of a man who neglects the philanthropic mission with which he has been entrusted by the government, thus causing the death of thousands of women and children, for the sake of his passionate love for a woman. The erotic parts of the film reach a high pitch of violence, culminating in a scene during which a flaming fir-tree, an enormous agricultural implement, an archbishop, a giraffe and some feathers are all flung out of a bedroom window at the top of a house. Other details include the ill-treating of a blind man, a dog being run over, a father killing his son on the spur of the moment, and an old woman having her face slapped. It is impossible to imagine what would happen were this film to be shown in England, even to a Film Society audience.

Salvador Dalí, a Catalan, brought with him into Surrealism an element until then almost unknown to it. His most important contribution to Surrealist experiment is his paranoiac method of criticism, first mention of which is to be found in an essay entitled *L'Ane a pourri*

[The Stinking Ass], which also appeared in the first number of *Le Surréalisme au service de la révolution*, and was subsequently published in Dalí's book *La Femme visible* (1930), a tribute to his wife (formerly Madame Eluard). 'Dalí has endowed Surrealism with an instrument of primary importance,' said André Breton in a lecture given at Brussels in 1934, 'in particular the paranoiac-critical method, which has immediately shown itself capable of being applied equally well to painting, poetry, the cinema, to the construction of typical Surrealist objects, to fashions, to sculpture, to the history of art and even, if necessary, to all manner of exegesis.'

The second number of *Le Surréalisme au service de la révolution*, which appeared later in the same year, contains poems, notes on current events, articles, etc., as before; but its most interesting feature is a text by Breton and Eluard, *L'Homme*, an extract from their book *L'Immaculée Conception* [The Immaculate Conception].

L'Immaculée Conception, published in December 1930, is the most significant Surrealist book of this period. The section called *The Possessions* consists of a series of simulations of various types of mental disease – mental debility, acute mania, general paralysis, delirium of interpretation and dementia præcox. 'The authors are particularly anxious,' says the preface,

> that these five essays, intended for the specialist as well as the lay reader, should be considered as constituting an absolutely sincere enterprise on their part; to suppose them in any way indebted to clinical texts, were it only to the extent of representing a more or less skilful pastiche of such texts, would be to presume them devoid of both necessity and efficacy. They have not been tempted by the charms of the picturesque into reproducing naïvely the phraseology that is considered, rightly or wrongly, as the least expressive of the objects to which it is applied; nor have they been satisfied to point the authentic curiosity of such a phraseology; on the contrary, they have shown that, given a state of *poetic* tension, the normal mind is capable of furnishing verbal material of the most profoundly paradoxical and eccentric nature, and it is possible for such a mind to harbour the main ideas of delirium without being permanently affected thereby or in any way jeopardised in its faculty of equilibrium.

There are other texts in the collection, the series *Man* (with the sub-titles: 'Conception', 'Pre-natal Life', 'Birth', 'Life', 'Death'); *The*

Mediations ('Force of Habit', 'Surprise', 'Nothing is Incomprehensible', 'The Sentiment of Nature', 'Love', 'The Idea of Becoming'); and *The Original Judgment*, a series of Surrealist proverbs. But the simulations of madness are the book's most important feature. 'The new phase of Surrealist experiment,' says Salvador Dalí,

> is given a really vital character and as it were defined by the simulations of mental diseases which in *The Immaculate Conception* André Breton and Paul Eluard have contrasted with their various poetic styles. Thanks to simulation in particular and images in general, we have been enabled, not only to establish communication between automatism and the road to the object, but also to regulate the system of interferences between them, automatism being thereby far from diminished but, as it were, liberated. Through the new relation thus established our eyes see the light of things in the external world. Thereupon, however, we are seized with a new fear. Deprived of the company of our former habitual phantoms, which only too well ensured our peace of mind, we are led to regard the world of objects, the objective world, as the true and manifested content of a new dream. (*The Object as Revealed in Surrealist Experiment*.)

L'Immaculée Conception and *La Femme visible* are typical examples of the new, active, attitude of Surrealism, as contrasted with its more or less passive attitude prior to the *Second Manifeste*. Dalí's system of paranoia, which I have already mentioned provisionally, demonstrates this. It should perhaps be explained that Dalí's use of the word *paranoia* does not signify 'persecution-mania' (as the word has come to mean almost exclusively in English); to him, persecution-mania is but an isolated example of paranoia, which is a mental state enabling the subject, with a superhuman swiftness of mind defying analysis, to draw from the objective world a concrete proof, or illustration, of his obsessions, or even of his transitory ideas. (Thus the subject of persecution-mania is continually able to draw proof from even the minutest details of other people's conversation, behaviour, etc., that he is being persecuted.) Dalí, for instance, is particularly preoccupied with a certain period of the painting of Picasso, and is seated at his desk about to write down his ideas about this; looking through his papers for some notes he comes across a picture-postcard that someone had quite carelessly sent to him some time before; it immediately appears to him to be a head by Picasso of the particular period about which he is going to write; closer examination proves, however, that the postcard, sideways up, is a photograph of an African village with natives sitting outside their huts. He then shows the postcard to his wife, without any explanation, and she also remarks the head; the maid, when questioned, gives the same reply; André Breton, when shown the postcard, declares it to be a portrait of the Marquis de Sade. Dalí claims that it is the paranoiac faculty that enables him to discover a head where there was, until he looked at it, only an African village. It is his paranoiac faculty, likewise, that enables him to give a most disconcerting interpretation to that famous painting of Millet's, *The Angelus*. It is paranoia that causes him to be constantly aware of the similarities between eating and making love, and to use innumerable 'edible' metaphors in his writings, and 'edible' images in his paintings, which are so full of erotic significance. As to those who say that Dalí is 'revolting', 'pathological', a 'muck-raker', and so on, they can very well be answered as follows:

> We cannot tell whether the three great images (*simulacres*) – excrement, blood and putrefaction – are not precisely concealing the *wished-for* 'treasure islands'. Being connoisseurs of images, we have long since learned to recognise the image of desire in images of terror, and even the reawakening of 'golden ages' in the shameful scatological images.

As every psychologist knows, the child loves his own excrement until he has been *taught* that it is dirty. It is only by fully understanding the arbitrary conventions, dogmas and laws that make up our civilisation that we can hope to begin to remedy it when the future society shall have been formed. Those who are always so ready to cry shame seldom reveal anything but their own predispositions.

★ ★ ★

The period 1930–31 saw also the appearance of *Artine*, by René Char, an author whose work has already been mentioned but which is somewhat difficult to describe very clearly. *Artine*, one might say, is a series of precise statements of vague thoughts inspired by an indefinable being.

> Sometimes a careless movement caused a head that was not mine to fall on Artine's throat. Then, the enormous mass of sulphur consumed itself slowly, without smoke, presence in itself and vibrating stillness.

Char, more that any other Surrealist writer, is concerned with clarity and careful detail. His collected writings were published in 1934 under the title *Le Marteau sans maître.*

It is interesting to mention as appearing at this time a short study of Paul Klee by René Crevel; for there is a misunderstanding to be cleared up here.

'He [Klee] is sometimes claimed by the French group known as Surréalistes', says Mr Herbert Read in his book *The Meaning of Art*, 'but if there is any question of relationship, it is the Surréalistes who derive from Klee, not Klee from the Surréalistes.' Now there is really no question of derivation at all, on either side; to suppose that would be to suppose a question of formal or æsthetic values. Surrealistic painting is not the *monopoly* of those artists who have devoted their whole energies to a systematic exploration of surrealist means of expression in the plastic domain, as Ernst, Dalí and Tanguy, for instance, have done; for surrealistic art has existed at all times and in all countries. Uccello, Bosch, Brueghel, Callot, El Greco, Goya, Blake, certain Pre-Raphaelites, Millet, Boecklin, Gustave Moreau, Odilon Redon, Aubrey Beardsley, James Ensor, Chagall, Pierre Roy, Henry Moore, to mention only a few, may all be regarded as surrealist artists, and nearly all the best so-called 'primitive' art may be regarded as surrealist also. All drawing, painting or sculpture that is not primarily or exclusively preoccupied with æsthetic form ('pure form' in the Roger Fry sense) or with the mere reproduction of the bald external appearance of logical reality, may legitimately be termed surrealist in the widest sense of the word. In the narrow sense of the word, admittedly, Surrealist art with a capital S should refer to the work of those who belong, or have belonged, to the specific Surrealist group. I draw the following names from the catalogue to the Surrealist exhibition held in Tenerife recently: Arp, Hans Bellmer, Victor Brauner, Giorgio de Chirico, Salvador Dalí, Oscar Domínguez, Marcel Duchamp, Max Ernst, Alberto Giacometti, Maurice Henry, Valentine Hugo, Marcel Jean, Dora Maar, René Magritte, Joan Miró, Meret Oppenheim, Pablo Picasso, Man Ray,

Jindřich Štyrský, Yves Tanguy. Eight nationalities are represented by those names, and there are still others.

The most scandalous thing about Surrealist art, from the point of view of the reactionary critics, is its tendency to do away with the old hierarchies of technical skill, 'fine drawing', craftsmanship, etc. Surrealism represents the point at which poetry and painting merge one into the other; and if poetry should be made by all, not one, then everyone should be able to make pictures, also. What upset the critics most about Dada was that plastic works by all the Dadaist writers were shown at the Dada exhibitions; what would happen to the artist's prestige, they wondered (and their own, reflected from it), if such a thing were to become more general? It would vanish; or the idea of what constitutes an artist would have to undergo a great change. All that is needed to produce a Surrealist picture is an unshackled imagination (and the Surrealists have often claimed that every human being is endowed with imagination, be he aware of it or not), and a few materials: paper or cardboard, pencil, scissors, paste, and an illustrated magazine, a catalogue or a newspaper. The marvellous is within everyone's reach.

Louis Aragon's *La Peinture au défi* (1930) constitutes a brilliant study of this aspect of Surrealism. He examines the whole question of the artist's prestige as a specialist and the means of undermining it, describing the progress of *collage* from the early days of Cubism to the recent experiments of René Magritte. There are, to begin with, the *papiers collés* of Picasso and Braque (newspaper, wallpaper, cigarette-packets), of which Tristan Tzara says:

> A shape cut out of newspaper and incorporated in a design or a picture unites the commonplace, a piece of everyday reality, with another reality constructed by the mind. The difference between various kinds of matter, that the eye is able to translate into tactile sensation, gives a new depth to the picture, in which weight is inscribed with mathematical precision on the symbol of volume, and its density, its taste, its consistency, place us before an unique reality created by the forces of the mind and of dream.

Ernst goes further than the Cubists and creates pictures entirely from pieces of other, ready-made, pictures by forgotten or anonymous artists. Miró uses nails, string, pieces of wood, as well as cutout papers (at his last exhibition there were pictures containing great brutal hanks of tarry rope). Francis Picabia once created a portrait entirely from blotting-paper, pen-nibs, wire, curtain-rings, needles and other objects; and one of Picasso's recent paintings contains pieces of straw and a real butterfly.

Other simple methods resembling *collage* include *frottage* (rubbing paper with charcoal over an uneven surface) as used by Max Ernst in his *Histoire naturelle*; written words incorporated in pictures, as used by René Magritte; and shadow-impressions on sensitised paper, as used by Man Ray (*Rayograms*).

All these experiments prelude the invention of the Surrealist object, first announced by Salvador Dalí in the third number of *Le Surréalisme au service de la révolution* (December 1931). Surrealist objects are of all sizes and of all degrees of complexity; they can generally be defined as *objects functioning symbolically*. Marcel Duchamp's cage of sugar, already mentioned; the bronze glove referred to in Breton's *Nadja*; certain pieces of 'sculpture' by Alberto Giacometti; certain works by Joan Miró – all these are Surrealist objects, concrete fantasies, irrational and perverse. Closer and more systematic attention to the idea of making such objects produced such things as a plaster head of a roaring lion with a fried egg in its mouth, a hairdresser's bust of a woman with a loaf of bread on her head surmounted by a metal inkstand representing Millet's *Angelus* (both by Dalí), and the following, by André Breton:

> An earthenware receptacle filled with tobacco on which are two long pink sugared almonds, is placed on a little bicycle-saddle. A polished wooden globe which can revolve in the axis of the saddle causes, when it moves, the end of this saddle to come in contact with two orange celluloid antennæ. The sphere is connected by means of two arms of the same material, with an hour-glass lying horizontally (so that the sand does not move), and with a bicycle-bell intended to ring when a green sugared almond is slung into the axis by means of a catapult behind the saddle. The whole affair is mounted on a board covered with woodland vegetation which leaves exposed here and there a paving of percussion-caps, and in one corner of the board, more thickly covered with leaves than the rest, there stands a small sculptured alabaster book, the cover of which is ornamented with a glaze photograph of the Tower of Pisa, and near this one finds, by moving the leaves, a cap which is the only one to have gone off: it is under the hoof of a doe.

These objects typify the more recent ideas of Surrealism, which conceive super-reality as existing in the material world, objectively, as well as subjectively in the automatic thought of the unconscious.

The third number of *Le Surréalisme au service de la révolution* appeared simultaneously with the fourth. In addition to Dalí's article on Surrealist objects, a commemoration of Hegel, an extract from André Breton's *Les Vases communicants* [The Communicating Vessels] and the usual poems and photos, it contains two particularly interesting articles by Louis Aragon, one entitled: *Lewis Carroll in 1931* (Aragon had just translated *The Hunting of the Snark*), and the other: *Surrealism and the Future of Revolution.* Number 4 contains another extract from *Les Vases communicants*, an article by René Crevel on *Patriotism and the Unconscious*, an extremely interesting and valuable *Essay on the Situation of Poetry* by Tristan Tzara, an astonishing *Reverie* by Dalí, and a few poems by Paul Eluard, including the following *Critique de la poésie*:

Of course I hate the reign of the bourgeois
The reign of cops and priests
But I hate still more the man who does not hate it
As I do
With all his strength.

I spit in the face of that despicable man
Who of all my poems does not prefer this *Critique de la poésie.*

But to return to Aragon's *Surrealism and the Future of Revolution*: it is in this article that we can observe the first signs of certain manœuvres that were shortly to lead to what was known as The Aragon Affair. In November 1930, Aragon had been to Russia, with Georges Sadoul, to represent Surrealism at the Kharkov Congress of Revolutionary Writers. Since then he had been in a most divided frame of mind; and although in this particular article he defends Surrealism very successfully against the criticisms that were levelled against the Surrealists in a resolution passed at this Congress, it is likely that the article did not express what Aragon really believed at that time. He was not yet anxious to break away from the Surrealists, because he was not yet sure of how he would be received by the orthodox Communists. A month later, however, the publication containing his poem Front Rouge [*Red Front*] was seized, and the events that followed provided him with an excellent opportunity to betray his former friends.

For the following account of The Aragon Affair I am indebted to the now defunct American review *Contempo*, and to Mr Jay du Von, the author of the article:[3]

> Louis Aragon's militant poem *Red Front* first appeared in the French edition of *Literature of the World Revolution*, a literary magazine published in Moscow by the International Union of Revolutionary Writers. After the edition had been on sale for nearly three months, the French police seized the remaining 350 copies in the bookshop of *L'Humanité*, the Communist daily paper in Paris, and Aragon's indictment followed.
>
> There were two charges, first, that of 'inciting to murder', based on the following lines in *Red Front*:
>
> *Fire on Leon Blum*
> *Fire on Boncour Frossard Deat*
> *Fire on the trained bears of the social democracy,*
>
> and second, that of 'provoking insubordination in the army', Aragon being held responsible not only for his own work, but as an editor of *Literature of the World Revolution*, for the contribution of V. Vichnevsky, *The Cavalry of Boudionny*, which appeared in the same number.
>
> Immediately after his indictment in January 1932, the Surrealist group, of which Aragon was one of the founders, sponsored a petition of protest which was circulated throughout Europe. The petition read, in part:
>
> > 'The indictment of Aragon for his poem *Red Front*, an indictment which exposes him to a sentence of five years in prison, is unprecedented in France.
> >
> > 'We protest against any attempt to give legal significance to a poetic work and demand the immediate withdrawal of the charge.'
>
> More than three hundred of the most important writers in Europe signed the petition and the support was obtained of the entire membership, over sixty thousand, of the French branch of the International Red Aid.
>
> Either as a result of this protest and a fear of the case becoming a *cause célèbre*, or because there seemed little hope of obtaining a conviction, the proceedings against Aragon were soon dropped.

---

[3] I have taken the liberty of altering Mr du Von's 'Super-realists' to 'Surrealists'.

2

However, the simple facts of the case are less interesting than some of the issues involved, including the refusals of certain prominent writers to sign the protest – and their reasons – and the repercussions of the affair among the Surrealists themselves.

As the Surrealists maintained in their protest, legal action against the author of an incendiary poem was without precedent in France and in proceeding against the author of a revolutionary article or against a distributor of pamphlets, the French government was making a new step in the direction of Fascist suppression. Yet it was exactly on this point that the greatest discussion was raised. On the 9th of February *L'Humanité* published an article calling attention to The Aragon Affair and asking for protests against all manifestations of bourgeois suppression:

> 'But we rigorously denounce the use of this affair by the Surrealists as a means of advertising themselves. Instead of fighting bourgeois suppression, the Surrealists are fighting only against the suppression of a lyric poem. They demand political immunity for poets and for poets alone. *We protest against any attempt to give legal significance to a poetic work*, they write.
>
> 'We cannot approve of the stand of those intellectuals who fail to stir when suppression strikes the workers and who move heaven and earth when it skims their precious persons.
>
> 'The Surrealist petition is a let-down pure and simple. In place of defending the content of the poem, they beat a retreat all along their *red front.* Their revolutionism is only verbal.
>
> 'They allow prosecution of *the forms of exact expression of thought*, but they want an exception made for poetry.
>
> 'The bourgeoisie, in its suppression of the revolutionary proletariat, sometimes strikes those who are clinging by chance to the working-class movement. Such is the meaning of *The Aragon Affair.*'

Somewhat the same stand was taken by Romain Rolland and several others in their refusal to sign the Surrealist petition. Other writers based their refusal to sign the protest on quite different reasons. One of the most violently reactionary was Charles Richet, who wrote: 'I know nothing of The Aragon Affair and have nothing to say on it. I only know that to defend the U.S.S.R. is to apologise for theft and assassination.' Hardly less reactionary but more tactful, André Gide refused to sign on the ground that he had been informed that the proceedings were in the nature of an inquiry, rather than a criminal action, and that in that case, he felt a protest was immature and likely to precipitate more serious action.

Other writers signed the protest, but qualified their signatures with personal amendments. André Lebey, for example, added the sentence, 'Long live Liberty, even after the Bolsheviks have triumphed and Aragon no longer desires it.' And Pierre Reverdy, an early Surrealist, appended the anarchistic note, 'Not placing any hope of relief for legitimate revolt in any form of government whatsoever, my name on this petition is a testimonial of friendly and fraternal solidarity.'

Bernard Brunius signed the petition, but wrote: 'The poem, surpassing in significance and portent its immediate content, becomes more subversive than any other form of expression. And as its value can be measured by its measure of effectiveness, it is not surprising to see it prosecuted. It is right that *art for the revolution* should expose the poet to the same risks as any other form of militant Communist activity.'

These and other objections to the protest were answered in a pamphlet by André Breton entitled *The Misery of Poetry*, which was published on the 5th of March by the Surrealists. In reviewing the stand of *L'Humanité* and the various refusals, Breton claimed that it was because of their desire to show clearly the accentuation of government suppression in France and to point out the exceptional character of the proceedings brought against Aragon, that the Surrealists had not sufficiently protested against the more general suppression which was being constantly exercised against political offenders. The Surrealists had taken it for granted, he explains, that their attitude in regard to it was beyond doubt, and that they had conceived their rôle as one of interesting the French intellectual circles, which had scarcely been touched by revolutionary propaganda, in the defence of intellectual freedom, and by so doing to participate more effectively in the struggle against general suppression.

3

At about the same time as the appearance of *The Misery of Poetry*, the French section of The International Union of Revolutionary Writers, an organisation to be known as The Association of Revolutionary Artists and Writers of France, was formed in Paris. Their manifesto, published in *L'Humanité*, called on all writers who claimed to be revolutionary to join the Association on a platform of dialectical materialism and the resolutions of the Kharkov Conference (November 1930).

As a result of the formation of The Association of Revolutionary Artists and Writers, the best elements separated themselves from the Surrealist group, including Aragon, Georges Sadoul, Buñuel, Pierre Unik and Maxime Alexandre, and *L'Humanité* published the following statement on the 10th of March:

> 'Our comrade Aragon has informed us that he had nothing to do with the publication of a brochure entitled *The Misery of Poetry* and signed by André Breton. He wishes to make it very clear that he disapproves of the entire brochure and the clamour which it is making over his name. And he condemns as incompatible with the class struggle, and consequently as objectively counter-revolutionary, the attacks which are contained in it.'

Aragon's repudiation of his old friend André Breton and the remaining members of the Surrealist group brought forth a violent attack on him in the form of a pamphlet entitled *Clown! (The End of The Aragon Affair)* and signed by René Char, René Crevel, Salvador Dalí, Paul Eluard, Max Ernst, Benjamin Péret, Yves Tanguy, André Thirion and Tristan Tzara. A few days later Paul Eluard also published a separate pamphlet in which he stated that he was completely severing relations with Aragon.

The last blast in The Aragon Affair was provided by a pamphlet signed by Pierre Unik and Maxime Alexandre. As participants in the Surrealist movement during many years, and as militant members of the Communist Party, they disagree with many of Breton's statements in *The Misery of Poetry*, but express their confidence in his ability to correct his errors. Aragon is censured for terming Breton a counter-revolutionist, and the authors regret that the signatories of *Clown!* have failed to rise above personal considerations. They conclude:

> 'The bourgeoisie answers with bullets the men forced into the streets by famine to demand work and bread. The kind of poets worthy of the name are allied with these men. Let the poets pay back stroke by stroke and not allow themselves to be buried under the rubbish of the society they are helping to destroy. Let the poets know that today they have a fatherland to defend!'

⋆ ⋆ ⋆

The question indirectly raised by this affair seems to be somewhat as follows: Is a militant Communist poet justified in writing any but propaganda poems or poems directly bearing on the working-class struggle? Yes, say the Surrealists; and No, say Aragon, Sadoul, Alexandre and a few others. (Both Buñuel and Pierre Unik appeared in Nos. 4 and 5 of *Le Surréalisme au service de la révolution* in 1933.) Mr du Von has not gone very closely into the arguments of Breton's *Misère de la poésie*, and I have not much space to do so here myself; but it should, I think, be mentioned that Breton supports his case for Surrealism by quoting Lenin as saying that the workers should be able to attain a more or less perfect knowledge of the whole field of thought, and that only a few pitiable intellectuals imagine that the workers want to read about factory life and the things they already know only too well. Surrealism being a form of psychological research in the domain of writing and painting, the Surrealists are helping to lay the foundations of a new, universal culture, and should not be expected to be immediately concerned, *in their researches*, with the practical facts of political struggle, though they have always shown themselves to be deeply concerned with it in their 'outside' declarations. Personally, I think that the Surrealists should be regarded as desirable 'fellow-travellers', and that the Communists are making a silly mistake in treating them either with scorn or suspicion simply because their work does not happen to be about strikes, hunger-marches or life in the distressed areas. They can in their own way do just as much good for the Revolution, ultimately, as the propaganda writers are doing in theirs.

As to *Red Front* itself, it is not a Surrealist poem: it is purely propaganda; strictly speaking, it is not 'poetry' at all, but prose written in the form of poetry – a prose statement, or argument, in poetic diction, enlivened with all the effects of imagery, metaphor and rhythmic rhetoric. André Breton's judgment of the poem is as follows:

> I say that this poem, on account of the way it is situated in Aragon's work, and in the history of poetry, corresponds to a certain number of formal determinations that are opposed to the isolation of such and such a group of words ('Bring down the cops Comrades') in order to exploit their literal meaning, when another such group ('The stars descend familiarly upon the earth') do not give rise to the question of literal meaning. Who would dare to pretend that in prose, in the course of an article, Aragon would have written 'Bring down the cops, Comrades', when such an injunction, otherwise without real importance, is contrary to the instructions of the Communist Party?

And Stephen Spender, reviewing in *New Verse* the English translation by e. e. cummings of the poem, said: 'If this type of propaganda has any effect at all, I do not see what that can be except to breed in people a superstitious belief in the necessity of murders and reprisals.'

A very valuable estimation of the whole question of Aragon's poetry, and of the relation between poetry and propaganda, is provided by a pamphlet published in 1934, *Les Paris sont ouverts* by Claude Cahun, a Communist writer, who, after examining poems written by Aragon *before* his 'conversion' and then poems written by him *afterwards*, comes to the conclusion that Aragon's later work represents a distinct deterioration, both in poetic and in revolutionary value. She also writes:

> The most revolutionary experience in poetry under the capitalist régime having been incontestably, for France and perhaps for Europe, the Dadaist-Surrealist experience, in that it has tended to destroy all the myths about art that for centuries have permitted the ideologic as well as economic exploitation of painting, of sculpture, of literature, etc. . . . (ex.: the *frottages* of Max Ernst which, among other things, have been able to upset the scale of values of art-critics and experts, values based chiefly on technical perfection, personal touch and the lastingness of the materials employed), this experience can and should serve the cause of the liberation of the proletariat. It is only when the proletarian has become aware of the myths on which capitalist culture depends, when he has become aware of what these myths and this culture mean for him and has destroyed them, only then will he be able to pass on to his own proper development. The positive lesson of this negating (*negatrice*) experience, that is to say its transfusion among the proletariat, constitutes the only valid revolutionary poetic propaganda.

By way of conclusion to this section, I should like to remark that all Marxist critics should beware of confusing *parlour* revolutionaries with *laboratory* (or work-room, studio, study) revolutionaries. Said Lenin: 'Without revolutionary theory, no revolutionary action.'

* * *

The year 1932 was also eventful for Surrealism in that it saw the appearance of several important works: André Breton's *Le Revolver à cheveux blancs* and *Les Vases communicants*, René Crevel's *Le Clavecin de Diderot*, Salvador Dalí's film scenario *Babaouo*, Paul Eluard's *La Vie immédiate*, Tristan Tzara's *Où Boivent les loups*, and the Surrealist number of *This Quarter*.

Incomparably the most important of these books is Breton's *Les Vases communicants*, in which he analyses the whole question of Surrealism and particularly the Surrealist study of dreams, demonstrating that inasmuch as the dream-life is an integral part of the whole life of man, it also can be investigated objectively and in the light of dialectical materialism. I do not think the book received in France the wide attention it deserved; but when a Czech translation was published recently in Prague, it was received with much enthusiasm, and the Marxist critic Zavis Kalandra wrote: 'This marvellously poetic Surrealist book is at the same time a scientific act . . . whose central importance to the progressive edification of Marxist-Leninist science should be apparent to all true Marxists.' It would be impossible to summarise Breton's lengthy arguments here, for the book is not a little complicated and much of its value rests on the careful documentation it contains. The title refers to the part played by Surrealism as a capillary thread, or tissue, 'assuring the constant exchange that should be brought about between the interior world and the exterior world, an exchange that necessitates the continuous interpenetration of the activity of waking and the activity of sleep.' It is to be hoped that an English translation of *Les Vases communicants* will appear before long.

Paul Eluard's *La Vie immédiate* placed him in the front rank of contemporary European poets, if *Capitale de la douleur* had not already done so. There is an absolute authenticity about everything that Eluard writes, an astonishing clarity of speech and image. If I have previously referred to the poetry of Eluard as 'pure', I should add, perhaps, that to seek disparagement of this term (so much abused in English criticism) is futile, since all authentic poetry is 'pure'; and by authenticity I mean: direct contact with the source of poetry, a source that may well be 'impure', since it is fed in its turn by all things in the world.

These two books and the five others mentioned above – two final numbers of *Le Surréalisme au service de la révolution*, containing notes on Hegel by Lenin, a series of remarkable enquiries on various objects, a collection of notes by Marcel Duchamp for his work *The*

Bride Stripped Bare by her Bachelors, Even, an article by Breton marking the centenary of Achim d'Arnim, the German author of *Contes bizarres*, and other features, such as *Enfances* and *La Belle en dormant*, two collections of poems by Georges Hugnet, who had just joined the Surrealist group, and *Les Pieds dans le plat* by René Crevel – all prove lively activity in the Surrealist movement during the period 1932–3.

In the next chapter we shall examine the most recent developments of Surrealism, and consider the possibilities that lie before it.

CHAPTER SIX

SURREALISM TODAY AND TOMORROW

Until recently the Surrealists had very seldom contributed to any but their own reviews; in 1933, however, they decided that in order to reach a new and wider public they would collaborate in the publication of *Minotaure*, a magnificently produced but somewhat expensive review, well known in this country. Whether they consider it an advantage to appear side by side with Paul Valéry and articles on Cézanne, I cannot say; but at any rate their work is now as well presented as it could be, with copious and finely produced illustrations. The seven or more numbers of *Minotaure* that have so far appeared have contained much valuable material by all the Surrealists. The articles by Breton ('Picasso in his Element', 'The Automatic Message', 'Beauty will be Convulsive'), and by Dalí ('Paranoiac-critical Interpretation of Millet's *Angelus*', 'Of the Terrifying and Comestible Beauty of Modern Style Architecture', 'The New Colours of Spectral Sex-Appeal'), are of especial interest. *Minotaure* has also contained a number of very valuable psychoanalytical studies by Dr Jacques Lacan, Dr Frois-Wittmann and others.

In 1934 the Surrealists also began to contribute to the Belgian review *Documents*, of which the number entitled *Intervention Surréaliste* is the most outstanding; it contains a manifesto occasioned by the riots of February 1934, headed *Appel à la lutte*, and signed by all the Surrealists as well as by a number of other writers and artists, including Jean-Richard Bloch, Fernand Léger and André Malraux. There is also an enquiry into the unity of anti-Fascist action, dated April 18th, addressed to all the chief representatives of the French workers; and a manifesto protesting against the nefarious treatment of Trotsky when passing through France.

There had been for some time a Surrealist group in Brussels, consisting of René Magritte, E. L. T. Mesens, Paul Nougé and Jean Scutenaire. They now began to manifest a more lively activity and to collaborate more closely with the Surrealist group in Paris. There has likewise been a Surrealist group in Belgrade for some years, another in Prague, another in the Canary Islands, another in Copenhagen.

In the summer of 1934, André Breton visited Brussels and delivered a lecture there, surveying all the most recent tendencies of the movement. The text has since been published under the title: *Qu'est-ce que le surréalisme?*

In April 1935, André Breton and Paul Eluard paid a visit to Prague, and delivered a series of lectures there to various left-wing organisations. They were extremely well received. As a result of this visit the first of a series of international Surrealist bulletins was published.

In May, André Breton and Benjamin Péret visited Tenerife, where a comprehensive Surrealist exhibition was held, and another bulletin has subsequently appeared.

On the return of Breton and Péret to Paris, a series of Surrealist *conférences* was announced, but owing to the tragic and obscure suicide of René Crevel, whose death was deeply regretted by all who knew him, they were put off until the autumn. Items of these *conférences* include:

> *Political Position of Art Today*, by Breton.
> *Mental Tests*, by Ernst.
> *Discourse on Religion*, by Péret.
> *The Surrealist Woman*, by Arp.
> Dalí will read his poem *I Eat Gala*, and will manipulate a strange living body.
> *Objective Chance as Pivot of the Surrealist Conception of Life*, by Breton.
> *Poetry's Evidence*, by Eluard.

From all this it will be seen that Surrealism has within the last year or so become an international movement, and is today more living than ever; within the near future we may expect developments on a scale unprecedented in the whole of its history. It is within the bounds of possibility that a Surrealist group may be founded shortly in London. André Breton and Paul Eluard have declared their intention of visiting England in the Spring of 1936, and there is talk of a large Surrealist exhibition being held at the same time. In all this can be seen something like a fulfilment of the words with which André Breton concluded his preface to the Surrealist number of *This Quarter* in 1932:

> *In the meantime* it does not at all appear to us impracticable to organise in the four corners of the earth a fairly extensive scheme of

resistance and experiment. This plan, as regards its mode of application, cannot be settled until there has been an interchange of the innermost desires of the live youth of all countries, and an estimate of the subversive forces which may be unleashed when it shall be applied at one given point. Owing to insufficient space at our disposal, this plan can only be barely hinted at. But beware! Enough if Surrealism is restored to its true perspective, and we shall not despair of seeing some day a storm *rising* from within this tea-cup.

* * *

In 1934 was published a *Petite Anthologie poétique du surréalisme*, edited and with an introduction by Georges Hugnet, containing examples of the work of eleven Surrealist writers and thirteen artists. The editor's introduction is particularly well done and constitutes one of the best short studies of Surrealism yet written. Georges Hugnet's long poem *Onan* was published in the same year, and so were André Breton's *Point du jour*, a collection of reprinted essays and articles covering a period of ten years, and his *L'Air de l'eau*, a new collection of poems; Paul Eluard's *La Rose publique*, new poems; Benjamin Péret's *De Derrière les fagots*, caustic buffoonery full of the most striking images, such as 'the strident cry of red eggs'; and Ernst's magnificent *collage* 'novel', *Une Semaine de bonté*.

Early in 1935 appeared Tristan Tzara's *Grains et issues*, described as an 'experimental dream', with copious notes. This book, with the possible exception of *L'Homme approximatif*, is Tzara's most important work. The first section of the book consists of prose texts, interspersed with poems, recreating once more the boundless illogical world of the dream and of uncontrolled thought; while the second section is a careful analysis of how and why this surreal world is created. On a Marxist basis Tzara examines the value of Surrealist poetic activity as the foundation of the 'culture' of the new society that will be brought about by the Revolution. Surrealism provides the germ of a new mentality; a new way of knowing the world, and incessantly opposes all the old pragmatisms that are struggling to maintain not only the old economic order but the old order of thought, with its unchangeable 'verities' and its lop-sided 'commonsense', as well.

Surrealism, as we have seen, is an activity of the mind, and cannot be limited to any one particular time or place. The Surrealist movement, the immediate product of certain currents of thought that happened to be more prevalent in nineteenth-century France than elsewhere, represents the very vigorous coherent effort of a number of men to develop this activity along experimental lines and to explore its widest possibilities. And there is every reason to believe that Surrealism, as a movement, is only just at the end of its earliest stages. If a really wide and properly organised international co-operation can be brought about, as there are signs that it shortly will be, Surrealism may become of even more importance to the twentieth century than it is already.

There will be, of course, objections to such a co-operation. In England, for instance, there will be many to protest that Surrealism is foreign to the national temperament, that it cannot grow here as it has no roots in English tradition. Such an objection could only result from a lack of understanding of what Surrealism *is*. As a matter of fact, there is a very strong Surrealist element in English literature; one need quote only Shakespeare, Marlowe, Swift, Young, Coleridge, Blake, Beddoes, Lear and Carroll to prove this contention. For a writer, or anyone else, to object to an attempt to establish Surrealist activity in England, on the grounds that this would mean an 'importation from Paris', is just as stupidly provincial as a doctor would be if he objected to the practice of psychoanalysis in England because it originated in Vienna. Surrealism itself, as it is today, is by no means wholly the product of previous French culture; there is a very strong element both of German and of Spanish thought in it, synthetising as it does the philosophy of Hegel, Feuerbach, Engels and Marx, and the distinctly southern 'lyricism' of painters such as Dalí, Miró and Picasso. For Surrealism transcends all nationalism and springs from a plane on which all men are equal.

It might be as well before concluding to summarise briefly the chief preoccupations of Surrealist research during the last ten years. These fall roughly into two categories: firstly, passive or subjective; secondly, active or objective.

To the first category belong automatism, spontaneous and 'pure' poetry, and the idea of the synonymity of poetry and dream. Parallel with these features, in the realm of art, may be placed *collage* and *frottage*, and the development of the idea of the element of anonymity and chance in artistic creation. From this idea of chance, or hazard (which really began in the days of Dada, with the production of poems by extracting words at random from a hat) to the paranoiac system introduced by Dalí, the development is much the same as that followed by Freud from his *Interpretation of Dreams* to *The Psychopathology of Everyday Life*, in which he advances the theory that accidents are very largely predetermined by psychic necessity. Objective hazard as the pivot of the Surrealist conception of life, is the subject to which Breton is at present devoting his attention; and Dalí has always contended that Surrealist objects 'take the form of desire'. No longer does a Surrealist await the message or the image to arise from the vast unconscious residue of experience; he actively imposes the image of his desires and obsessions upon the concrete, daylight world of objective reality; he actively takes part in 'accidents' that reveal the true nature of the mechanism that is life far more clearly than 'pure psychic automatism' could.

In addition to all this we must take into consideration the unchanging political position of the Surrealists in opposing bourgeois society, attacking religion, patriotism and the idea of family, and in declaring their belief in the principles of Communism and their solidarity with the proletariat of all countries.

In conclusion, tribute should be paid to André Breton, whose energy, enthusiasm and powers of leadership have been and are still of inestimable value not only to the Surrealist movement but to all those taking part in it. He is one of the most remarkable men of his time, and his influence will long continue to make itself felt in modern thought.

It is my hope that the reader will have realised by now that Surrealism is not simply a way of writing or of painting, but a school of thought that may very well be playing a rôle of historical importance. The great task of this century is that of revising the old scales of value in every field, of destroying worn-out customs and institutions and of constructing a form of society in which men may be able to make full use of all their faculties. Few poets – and poets, though still unacknowledged, continue to be the legislators of the world – have set about this task with so great a thoroughness as have the Surrealists. Already they have succeeded in widening and deepening the total of human experience.

TRANSLATIONS

ANDRÉ BRETON

'ON THE SAINT-GENEVIÈVE MOUNTAIN . . .'

On the Saint-Geneviève mountain there is a wide drinking-place where, when night falls, all the disturbing beasts and surprising plants that still exist in Paris come to refresh themselves. You might think it would dry up did you not see, on examining things rather closer, a little red trickle that nothing can stanch. What precious blood, then, continues flowing in this place so that the feathers, down, white hairs and declorophyled leaves that it sets going turn back when they reach the only end that is visible? What princess of royal blood consecrates herself thus after her disappearing on the entreaty of all the most sovereignly tender flora and fauna of this country? What saint with apron of roses has made this divine extract flow into the veins of stone? Every evening the marvellous mould more beautiful than a breast is opened and new lips and the refreshing virtue of rose-blood join the whole of the surrounding sky, while on a boundary-stone shivers a young child counting the stars; soon it will bring back its herd from the millenary manes, from the archer or water-arrow who has three hands, one for extracting, the other for caressing, the other for shading or directing, from the archer of my days to the Alsatian dog who has one blue and one yellow eye, the dog of the anaglyphs of my dreams, the marshes' faithful companion.

(From: *Manifeste du surréalisme: poisson soluble*
[Manifesto of Surrealism: Soluble Fish], 1924)

ANDRÉ BRETON

THE SPECTRAL ATTITUDES

I attach no importance to life
I pin not the least of life's butterflies to importance
I do not matter to life
But the branches of salt the white branches
All the shadow bubbles
And the sea-anemones
Come down and breathe within my thoughts
They come from tears that are not mine
From steps I do not take that are steps twice
And of which the sand remembers the flood-tide
The bars are in the cage
And the birds come down from far above to sing before these bars
A subterranean passage unites all perfumes
A woman pledged herself there one day
This woman became so bright that I could no longer see her
With these eyes which have seen my own self burning
I was then already as old as I am now
And I watched over myself and my thoughts like a night-watchman
    in an immense factory
Keeping watch alone
The circus always enchants the same tramlines
The plaster figures have lost nothing of their expression
They who bit the smile's fig
I know of a drapery in a forgotten town
If it pleased me to appear to you wrapped in this drapery
You would think that your end was approaching
Like mine
At last the fountains would understand that you must not say Fountain
The wolves are clothed in mirrors of snow
I have a boat detached from all climates
I am dragged along by an ice-pack with teeth of flame
I cut and I cleave the wood of this tree that will always be green
A musician is caught up in the strings of his instrument
The skull and crossbones of the time of no childhood story

Goes on board a ship that is as yet its own ghost only
Perhaps there is a hilt to this sword
But already there is a duel in this hilt
During the duel the combatants are unarmed
Death is the least offence
The future never comes

The curtains that have never been raised
Float to the windows of houses that are to be built
The beds made of lilies
Slide beneath the lamps of dew
There will come an evening
The nuggets of light become still underneath the blue moss
The hands that tie and untie the knots of love and of air
Keep all their transparency for those who have eyes to see
They see the palms of hands
The crowns in eyes
But the brazier of crowns and palms
Can scarcely be lit in the deepest part of the forest
There where the stags bend their heads to examine the years
Nothing more than a feeble beating is heard
From which sound a thousand louder or softer sounds proceed
And the beating goes on and on
There are dresses that vibrate
And their vibration is in unison with the beating
When I wish to see the faces of those that wear them
A great fog rises from the ground
At the bottom of the steeples behind the most elegant reservoirs of
 life and of wealth
In the gorges which hide themselves between two mountains
On the sea at the hour when the sun cools down
Those who make signs to me are separated by stars
And yet the carriage overturned at full speed
Carries as far as my last hesitation
That awaits me down there in the town where the statues of bronze
 and of stone have changed places with statues of wax
Banyans banyans.

(From: *Le Revolver à cheveux blancs* [The White-Haired Revolver], 1932)

RENÉ CHAR

THREE POEMS

POETS

'The circle is a figure surrounded by a circular line.' RAYMOND LULLE

The melancholy of illiterates in the mystery of bottles
The imperceptible disquiet of cartwrights
Pieces of money in the slender vase

In the cockle-shell of the anvil
Dwells the lonely poet
Great wheelbarrow of the swamps.

THE PUMA OF THE MARQUIS DE SADE

to MAURICE HEINE

The unsullied blood takes pleasure in the rose-garden
Has mental contact with the torch
So full of juice is the caressed mane
The smell ascending to near a colony of delights
Greets the secluded wishes
Dominion of the unclad rose
Like frost under the black water sleeps the fatal toad.

LOVE

The neuter hands of stoic skeletons to stroke your hair
Black as liquorice are the months of scarcity
You shut your eyes upon the quarry of unworkable ochre
You suck up through a hunting spear the subterranean water
You are hypnotised in space for the leaf's sake
To the drawing near of the invisible serpent
The foxglove's pith.

(From: *Le Marteau sans maître* [The Masterless Hammer], 1934)

(Translated by RUTHVEN TODD)

RENÉ CHAR

FATAL SLEEP

The animals with heads like ships surround the face of the woman that I love. The mountain weeds wither under the eyelids' period of quiet. The memory of the man realises without difficulty what he believes to be the experience of his most hopeless dreams whilst at the inclination of his mirrors he continues to drain the unattainable water. And the ashes' thought?

(The man denies himself disbelief in the sincerity of the letters written to him while a child by an unknown woman. This woman unveiled for him the prophetic side of his writing. The precise black colour of the future authorised him to express a preference: he will kiss a sand-pit that is the damnation of meteorites; these virtuosi of transition readily forget their edible heads on the meat-safe shelf, at twilight.)

(Translated by RUTHVEN TODD)

SALVADOR DALÍ

LOVE AND MEMORY (Fragment)

There are things as still as a loaf.
In the endearing districts
but not excessively endearing
demarked very quickly and politely
predisposed to colonial influences
a mask
gathered in like a loan
was
practically
upset
without getting mixed up
with
this colonial district
where
there were
several departmental
wands
Other things, indeterminate and
departmental things
functioning as
bread
well-browned bread
resembling weeping
the weeping
resembling
the picture of a nest
reproduced in three colours
the nest resembling
the word-emblem
I shall carry furiously
whether conditionally
or not
the colonially
masked things

united
whether very appreciably
or not
by a single edge
or
by general cheek-bones
or
by several ensembles
or
by a balanced thing
or
by demi-things
or
by turned things
or
by a handle
or
by handles
or
by a thing placed
near a piece of needlework
headed by yards and crusts
or
by my sister's picture.

(1931)

PAUL ELUARD

'AT THE END OF A LONG VOYAGE . . .'

At the end of a long voyage I always see this corridor once more, this mole, this warm shadow to which the foam of the sea prescribes pure breezes like tiny children, I always see once more the room where I came to break with you the bread of our desires, I always see once more your undressed pallor which unites in the morning with the disappearing stars. I know I am going to close my eyes again in order to rediscover the colours and conventional forms which allow me to approach you. When I open them again it will be so as to find in a corner of the room the corruptible pickaxe-sleeved parasol which causes me to doubt fine weather, the sun, life, for I no longer love you in full daylight, I regret the time when I was setting out to discover you, and also the time when I was blind and dumb before the incomprehensible universe and the incoherent system of agreement that you were suggesting to me.

Have you not sufficiently borne the responsibility of that frankness which obliged me to be continually turning your own whims against you?

What haven't you given me to think about? I now come no longer to see you except in order to reassure myself of the great mystery which still constitutes the absurd duration of my life, the absurd duration of a night.

The boats all sail away when I arrive, the storm recoils before them. A shower sets free the obscure flowers, their blossoming begins again and strikes once more the woollen walls. You are never sure of anything, I know, but the idea of falsehood and the idea of an error are so much stronger than we are. It is so long since the obstinate door refused to give in, so long since the monotony of hope fed boredom, so long since your smiles were tears.

We have refused to allow spectators to enter, for there is nothing to see. Remember, when you are alone, the empty stage without any scenery or actors or musicians. Thus it is: the theatre of the world, the worldly stage, and we two, we no longer know what it means. We two – I insist on those words, for at the ports of call on those long voyages we made separately, I know it now, we were really together, we really were, we were, we. Neither you nor I know how to add the time when we were apart to the time when we were together, neither you nor I know how to take one away from the other.

Each one a shadow, but in the shadow we forgot that it was so.

(From: *La Vie immédiate* [The Immediate Life], 1932)

PAUL ELUARD

WHAT THE WORKMAN SAYS IS NEVER TO THE POINT

A winter all branchy and hard as a corpse
A man on a bench in a street that escapes from the crowd
And is filled up with solitude
Makes way for the banal machinery of despair
For its mirrors of lead
For its baths of pebbles
For its stagnant statues
Makes way for the neglect of good
For the tattered memories of truth
Black light old conflagration
With hair lost in a labyrinth
A man who mistook the landing the door and the key
So as to know more so as to love more.

Where does the landscape begin
At what time
Where then does woman come to an end
The evening balances over the town
The evening rejoins the stroller in his bed
The naked stroller
Less greedy for a virgin breast
Than for the shapeless star that gives suck to the night.

There are indescribable demolitions sadder than a farthing
But nevertheless the sun escapes from them singing
While the sky dances and makes its honey
There are deserted walls where the idyll blossoms
Where the flaking plaster
Cradles mingled shadows
A rebellious fire a fire of veins
Beneath the only wave of lips
Take hands see eyes
Take the landscape by force.

Behind the palace behind the rubbish-heaps
Behind the chimneys and the cisterns
In front of man
On the esplanade that unrolls a coat of dust
By fever drawn
It is the invasion of fine days
A plantation of blue daggers
Beneath the opened eyelids in a crowd of leaves
It is pleasure's heavy harvest.

The flower of flax breaks the masks
The faces are washed
By the colour that knows the extent.

The clear days of the past
Their barred lions and their eagles of pure water
Their thunder of pride inflating the hours
With the blood of enchained dawns
All across the sky
Their diadem shrivelled on the mace of a single mirror
Of a single heart.

But now far deeper among the abolished roads
This song that holds the night
This song that deafens and blinds
That offers its arm to ghosts
This denying love
That struggles in anguish
With well-soaked tears
This torn disabled twisted ridiculous dream
This fallow harmony
This begging horde.

For she has desired only gold
And love's perfection
Her whole life long.

(From: *La Rose publique* [The Public Rose], 1934)

GEORGES HUGNET

POEM

The chrysalis says she is the fern's perfection,
chance is being's will,
the hatchway is a grain of salt on a frigate's sail,
the doors are pieces of shadow, the drawers are at play,
the triangles are earthen,
indolence is reddish, the lama's nose is a window,
good-morning chases a fly on to the ceiling,
the walls are the halt of the ultramarine and the roof is a pump,
your face does not exist,
my love is well polished,
the sea interrogates its beaches secretly,
living is not following a mirror's movements as best one can,
the winged ant is an ear,
tears are the beggars who roll to the bottom of ponds,
a room is the bother of leaving it,
entering it is to allow oneself everything, I wish you were chilly,
desolation is a bunch of papers,
the wind is a hand, the hand a raspberry,
when the sea comes up, chance threads a needle,
the shine of your fingernails is echoed by the apples,
looking is not for much more than a pillow-case,
habit is the eye and speaking is black,
if I ask myself questions I dress in beetle,
reason is the same as fear:
the little green spot that shakes about in the red sea,
blood is a sculpture,
a book or the wherewithal to die,
the addressee of a letter is an island-shaped stain,
your hair is an ant-hill, a medlar-tree before a cheval-glass,
presence and solitude are two beans in a black room,
two beans facing one another,
to give shade one turns on the same switch
that immortalises the last cigarette of a man condemned to death
and there you have the beheading of human justice,

sleeping is a word
and oracle a mania; egg, awakened dreamer,
neither humility nor vanity is my strong point,
the tree is a dandyism,
a tower goes down the river, Barbary fig,
you are my only pride, I am only pride before you,
the images are not sufficiently distant,
the giraffe is the year's longest eyelash,
one must renounce all commentary,
unlearn all that was learnt
and live only in the incredible
in order to live.

BENJAMIN PÉRET

THREE POEMS

AND SO ON

A kick in the pants once more
and the empty sardine-tin thinks itself holy
A kick with the heel on the jaw
and it is a divinity
which swims in pure honey
not caring about protozoons
sea-horses
or heavenly pebbles that flutter from eye to eye
and carry reason
with a little sauce and some broken teeth
into the society of cabbage-stumps
who no longer know what to do with their heads
since thick waters stifle in furs.

HONEST FOLK

The quarrel between the boiled chicken and the ventriloquist
had for us the meaning of a cloud of dust
which passed above the city
like the blowing of a trumpet
It blew so loudly that its bowler-hat was trembling
and its beard stood up on end
to bite off its nose
It blew so loudly
that its nose cracked open like a nut
and the nut spat out
into the far distance
a little cow-shed
wherein the youngest calf
was selling its mother's milk
in sausage-skin flasks
that its father had vulcanised.

(From: *De derrière les fagots* [From Behind the Faggots], 1934)

THE FLEAS OF THE FIELD

Work with all your strength
Work on the land the streets the docks
and sow there what you will
paving-stones smoke or bottles
but work work like a lunatic
and dung the stones
that they may sprout flags
even red ones
The rains and the winds will bless you
if you put the hands of a watch to your ears
and the harvest will be good as your wife's stew.

Work your own field and all the others
with your feet and with your nose
Break down the hedges like a bull
while singing
In the Revolution
there was a worker
who clinked with his spade
he had only one head and two arms
four feet and two eyes
one ear and three teeth
but he was a worker
who did not waste his time.

(From: *Le Grand Jeu* [The Great Game], 1928)
(Translated by RUTHVEN TODD)

TRISTAN TZARA

THE APPROXIMATE MAN (Fragment)

the mountains' whooping-cough charring the escarpments of the
gorges
in the pestiferous buzzings of autumnal aqueducts
cultivation of the gratuitous sky, communal ditch snapped at by so
many crystalline pastures
the languages of nudes brief apparitions of messengers
in their annunciatory tufts of supreme clamours and obsessions
the restless underground chemical-works lagging like songs
the swiftness of rain its raw telegraphic tingling of ruminating shell
pick-axes' crude punctures whence frothing lye emerges
broken on all the landscapes and on the tricks of the jeering valleys
tempting the nations
the godless promenades of water-courses
the temerity of their exploits against the seated dusk of clay
the forgetting of captive essences drowned in the forgetting of
numbers and ferries
and the fibrous dungeons heaped with corn-ears and bells
where spinners of cares disappear in the darkness quaking with
scythes
and open visual capsules at the end of the sexual icicles of ghosts
the rawness of the kernels of stone walls climbed by a thousand
fingers
interlacing themselves with dandelion tresses
and the pathetic balancing of temperatures raked by the excessive
gaze

your complacences set up in me too sweet a meandering of easy and
sleeping oracle
and flinty in my clothes of slate I have devoted my watching
to the torment of the oxydised desert
and to the robust accession of fire

crushed against the basaltic dumbness of the ibises
hanging from the bridles of underground rivers
a prey to mad forests of hydras
where the thick summers' sermons gargle dreamy rivalries
night swallows us up and casts us out to the other end of the lair
moving beings whom the eyes' grammar has not yet defined upon
 the area of tomorrow
slow coral encirclings
disgorge the high forks of rocky wills
the cantles of your heart a heavy weather of gravel
and how many barracks in the shelter of your forehead have written
 the wide mourning of moss on the breast
falling in ruin of masses of futures
covered with embroiled loads mixed with the lianas' clumsy
 ambushes
where the ridges of troubles and fishes let opaque death and tresses
 trickle through them

we were going on to moors made sweet by attention
sweetly attentive to the monotonous jolts of the phenomena
that the ungrateful exercise of the infinite printed on the blocks of
 perception
but the scaly structures of scarce opinions
on the damp infinity of diadems – the fields –
disdains truths' palpable pulp
with a ready favour of quickened punishment
axes were hacking among roan laughter
and the disks of the hours flew to the attack
burst in the head of the aerial herds
it was our reasons lying fallow that were stemming their diaphanous
 turbulence
and the knotty trajects that they traced in time
had a tentacular incarnation in the constraint of clay

there we abandoned the pleasure and the dogma of the spectacle
and sacrificed to other impulses the goldenbrown desire that its fruit
 brought to us

mow down, diamantine insistences, the vain landscapes elaborated by my senses
deaf upright hallucinating distrust
on the turntable of my being all the roads are open to you
carry away what the drunkenness of reproach has not yet known how to throw down
and everything that I could once understand and in which I believe no more
and the clot of those things that I could not understand which rises to my throat
and the seawrack tanned by the implacable toil of the depths
and the flower of the triangle incised on the pupil
and the battle lost by my breath on the stiff white page
and the osmosis of odious thoughts
and the sorrows riddled by persistent sowings of seduction
and the voluted hut of dust
and that of the lost soul
and so many others and so many others
recovered or ill
for flinty in my clothes of slate I have devoted my watching
to the torment of the oxydised desert
to the robust accession of fire

hands strangely secluded from clusters of transparent hands
mingle with the dominoes of stars upon the savanna they are sheep
and the barks of crushed clouds of nautical odours linger
on the table of the sky encumbered with eucharistic games
what games what savage joys feed with disarray your proceeding into the sky of acclimatisation
where wild beasts and planets roll entwined with opium eyes
stretched out from end to end of the aquarium your heart so luminously slashed with silence
dedicated to the careful tricks of the blades
incrusted with rebellious drops of wine and with impious words
drinks in the coming and going of ecstasies in the verbal congestion whose typhoon stigmatises your forehead

carven henceforth is the prow of the ramparts according to the way
they swim
but now your eyes guide the cyclone
lofty tenebrous intention
and at sea as far as the limits of the bird vigils
the wind coughs as far as the limit where death discharges
promethean cataracts of echoes thunder into our benumbed
consciousness
it means suffering when the earth remembers you and shakes you off
beaten and poor village dog you wander
and ceaselessly return the point of departure unconsoled with the
word
a flower in the corner of your mouth a phthisic flower knocked about
by the rough necropolis
tons of wind are poured out into the deaf citadel of fever
a skittle at the mercy of a thoughtless movement what am I
an unconsoled point of departure to which I return smoking the
word in the corner of my mouth
a flower beaten by the rugged fever of the wind
and flinty in my clothes of slate I have devoted my watching
to the torment of the oxydised desert
to the robust accession of fire

when the ramifications of chance fasten on to the ropes by means of
their smile
when your heart is called – there where the solid bits sink down
dusty and sour moth – dull intimacy – what do I know – shipyard of
night
when the beaten-up jar full of whistlings of sharp-edged reptiles' frill
in which rave the madreporic solicitations of male inclemencies
rumbles at length and moans
a slow furnace of invincible constancy – man –
a slow furnace rises up from the bottom of your slow gravity
a slow furnace rises up from the valley of the chief glaciers
a slow furnace of unspeakable alloys
a slow furnace which reaches the hearths of the lucid emotions
a wide furnace rises up from the enslaved coughings of fortresses
a slow fire quickens to the gaping dread of your strength – man –

a fire quickens the heights of nymph where the coastings of stratus
have earthed-up the taste of gulf
a fire that climbs up the suppliant ladder as far as the stains of the
limitless gestures
a fire that barks out shouts of regret above the hypocritical suggestions
of possibility
a fire that escapes from the muscular seas where plays the unconscious
with speedy flights – man –
a man who shakes with the indefinable presumptions of mazes of
fire
a fire that warps the swelling mass of revolt of letters – folds itself up
harmony – may this word be banished from the feverish world I visit
of ferocious affinities dug out of nothingness covered with murders
that yells at not breaking down the sobbing barrier of shreds of
flamingoes
for the fire of anger varies the animation of the subtle wrecks
according to the stuttering modulations of hell
that your heart exhaustedly recognises among the dizzy volleys of
stars
and flinty in my clothes of slate
I have devoted my watching to the oxydised desert of torment
to the robust accession of its flames

(1929)

ANDRÉ BRETON and PAUL ELUARD

FORCE OF HABIT

The table is placed in the dining-room; the taps give out clear water, soft water, tepid water, scented water. The bed is as large for two as for one. After the bud will come the leaf and after the leaf the flower and after rain fine weather. Because it is time, the eyes open, the body stands up, the hand stretches out, the fire is lit, the smile contends with night's wrinkles for their unmalicious curve. And they are the clock's hands that open, that stand up, that stretch out, that set light to themselves and mark the hour of the smile. The sun's ray goes about the house in a white blouse. It's going to snow again, a few drops of blood are going to fall again at about five o'clock, but that'll be nothing. Oh! I was frightened, I suddenly thought there was no longer any street outside the window, but it is there just the same as ever. The chemist is even raising his metal shutters. There will soon be more people at the wheel than at the mill. Work is sharpened, hammered, thinned down, reckoned out. Once more the hand takes pleasure in finding the security of sleep in the familiar implement.

Provided that it lasts!

The mirror is a marvellous witness, changing all the time. It gives evidence calmly and with power, but when it has finished speaking you can see that it has been caught out again over everything. It is the current personification of verity.

On the hairpin-bend road obstinately tied to the legs of him who assesses today as he will assess tomorrow, on the light bearings of carelessness, a thousand steps each day espouse the steps of the vigil. They have come already and they will come again without being invited. Each one has passed that way, going from his joy to his sorrow. It is a little refuge with an enormous gas-jet. You put one foot in front of the other and then you are gone.

The walls cover themselves with pictures, the holidays sift themselves with bouquets, the mirror covers itself with vapour. As many light-houses on a stream and the stream is in the vessel of the river. Two eyes the same, for the use of your single face – two eyes covered with the same ants. Green is almost uniformly spread over the plants, the wind follows the birds, no one risks seeing the stones die. The result is not a broken-in animal but an animal trainer. Bah! It is the indefeasible order of a ceremony already, on the whole, so very gorgeous! It is the repeating pistol which makes flowers appear in vases and smoke in the mouth.

Love, in the end, is well satisfied with seeing night clearly.

When you are no longer there, your perfume is there to search for me. I only come to get back the oracle of your weakness. My hand in your hand is so little like your hand in mine. Unhappiness, you see, unhappiness itself profits from being known. I let you share my lot, you cannot not be there, you are the proof that I exist. And everything conforms with that life which I have made to assure myself of you.

– What are you thinking about?

– Nothing.

(From: *L'Immaculée Conception* [The Immaculate Conception], 1930)

APPENDIX 1

Illustrations

The illustrations in the 1935 edition were as follows:

Valentine Hugo, *Portraits of Paul Eluard, André Breton, Tristan Tzara, René Crevel* (in course of execution)

Hans Arp, *Dancer (string)* (1927)

Giorgio de Chirico, *Il giorno di festa* [The Fête Day] (1914)

Salvador Dalí, *Sevrage du meuble-aliment* [The Weaning of Furniture-Food] (1934)

Max Ernst, *Le Lion de Belfort* (collage) (1934)

Alberto Giacometti, *The Palace at 4 A.M.* (1923; now at MoMA, New York): sculpture, photographed by Brassaï

René Magritte, *Au seuil de la liberté* [On the Threshold of Freedom] (1930; now at the Museum Boymans-van Beuningen, Rotterdam)

Salvador Dalí and Luis Buñuel, from the film *Un Chien andalou* [An Andalusian Dog] (1929)

Joan Miró, *Personatge tirant una pedra a un ocell* [Person Throwing a Stone at a Bird] (1926; now at MoMA, New York)

Pablo Picasso, *Dinard* (1928)

Man Ray, *Dust Raising* (1920): photograph of part of Marcel Duchamp's work *The Bride Stripped Bare by her Bachelors, Even*, in its unfinished state

Yves Tanguy, *I Am Waiting for You* (1935), photographed by Man Ray

APPENDIX 2

Back cover of 1935 edition

André Breton's 'list of writers, philosophers and others, past and present, who may in one way or another be considered as Surrealists' (see page 58).

What is Surrealism?

IT IS *the cowl of the hotel mouse dear to Victor Brauner*
IT IS *the Fifth Book of Magic by René Char*
IT IS *the vessel of which René Crevel becomes the master, amidst the tempest, by closing his eyes*
IT IS *the entrance of Salvador Dalí holding the Philosophers' Stone between two raised fingers*
IT IS *the least caprice of Marcel Duchamp*
IT IS *the sparkling of Paul Eluard's glass*
IT IS *Max Ernst, long after the invention of silk, drawing Ariadne's thread from the cocoon of mimetic insects*
IT IS *the struggle of Alberto Giacometti with the Angel of Invisibility who has made an appointment with him among the blossoming apple-trees*
IT IS *Georges Hugnet's kiss on the mouth of the Beauty*
IT IS *the vision of Valentine Hugo, pierced by the cry of Sisteron*
IT IS *the cuckoo's egg laid in the nest (whose brood is lost) with the complicity of René Magritte*
IT IS *re-learning to read by means of E. L. T. Mesens' star-alphabet*
IT IS *Paul Nougé's great mystery lesson*
IT IS *the handsomeness of Benjamin Péret while listening to words of family, religion and patriotism*
IT IS *the mirror bent in Man Ray's arms*
IT IS *the appearance of Yves Tanguy, his hair done in the* paradisier grande émeraude *style*
IT IS *the violet holding back the cantharides hats of Tristan Tzara*

André BRETON

INDEX

The names in italics indicate those who belonged to the Surrealist group